The Emperor's Clothes

RYAN DARWISH MBA, CFP®, CLU, CHFC
A FEE-ONLY NAPFA REGISTERED INVESTMENT ADVISOR

THE EMPEROR'S CLOTHES

A MOSAIC LOOK AT THE MEGA-TRENDS AFFECTING YOUR INVESTMENT AND FINANCIAL PLANNING DECISIONS

2007

The Emperor's Clothes

TABLE OF CONTENTS

CHAPTER ONE
The Need for a Global Perspective

Does financial planning and investment decision-making, for you, amount to little more than rearranging the deck chairs on the <u>Titanic</u>? As a Certified Financial Planner and Registered Investment Advisor, my professional observations and experiences over sixteen years have lead me to believe that most people are exposed to being financially blind-sided by clearly definable mega-trends. These are events that we hear about regularly. In fact, we hear about them so regularly that they become little more than background noise. That is, until they become crises when we experience the impact of these events in our personal lives.

It does not take a genius to recognize that our global environment is volatile and worrisome. We live in a global environment that is perpetually either on the edge of war or is one in which war is actually being waged. Oil, the energy foundation of modern civilization, and other natural resources face a growing demand, at a time of diminishing supply, from the rapidly emerging economies of China and India. Our Federal and State budget deficits extend without end. In the United States, and many other developed countries, we have aging populations with growing indebtedness and diminishing savings. They will need health care and other social resources at a time when the ability to pay for these services are impaired and the pension promises of many companies are turning out to be empty. Greed and corruption regularly undermine whatever faith may be left in the financial system.

The feelings of safety and security that we have been privileged to experience in our country, because of America's preeminent stature in the world of the twentieth century, are rapidly being eroded.

Why is the <u>Titanic</u> a parallel?

Ironically, during the tragic episode of the sinking of that supposedly unsinkable ship, many people busied themselves with meaningless activities in the face of what they were to experience. Perhaps it was psychological denial of an inevitable unpleasant future, or perhaps it was lack of awareness. A review of the manifests of the <u>Titanic's</u> lifeboats indicates that many of them were not filled to capacity when they left the <u>Titanic</u>. Many more lives could have been saved had the available resources been more fully used. Had more people recognized and acknowledged the gravity of their circumstances. it is likely that the time and energy spent engaging in meaningless activities could have been directed towards creating a higher survival rate than that which actually occurred. This is a book about recognizing and acknowledging the gravity of the global events affecting our personal financial lives. It is not only about financial survival. It is also about accepting that despite an extremely hazardous financial and investment environment, unique opportunities will also arise which will offer us the chance to do extremely well with our investments. If we are to do this, however, we must look through the veil of accepted stale thinking and self-serving commercialized rhetoric that passes for conventional wisdom.

Many people have been encouraged to believe that some mechanical process, formula, or computer program will guide them to financial security. These people will likely find it to be uncomfortable to have to think about the complexity of our global environment and the implications some of these global mega-trends will have in our personal financial lives. For those individuals willing to take this journey, this book will serve as a guide to assist in bringing into focus that which appears to be unalterable financial impacts of the mega-events that are rapidly heading towards us.

Most people are so involved in the day to day activities of their daily lives that they are missing the larger picture of how the playing out of major global economic and geopolitical events is likely to affect their financial futures. Unfortunately, the same can be said for many of the advisors that offer help and guidance in these areas, as well as many of the media commentators. While this type of planning is not totally without value, neglecting to take into consideration the events that continually shape our financial lives leaves an unstable foundation upon which to base our financial futures. It also fails to use the opportunity to be proactive in the face of impending adverse circumstances. In the best of circumstances there are enough uncertainties about the future. In our current geopolitical and global economic environment we are looking at a structural change in the world as we have known it. Failing to recognize and consider the possible outcomes of these events, and their effects on our personal financial situations, will severely compromise our future circumstances.

Over the last sixteen years I have worked with, counseled, and taught hundreds of individuals about personal financial issues. Through thousands of hours of continuing education, collaboration with attorneys, CPA's, and investment professionals, I have come to the conclusion that most advice, and thinking, neglects to consider one or more global issues likely to impact their client's lives and is based on parochial viewpoints of the world. In the past this has proven adequate. America's rise to affluence and global preeminence during the twentieth century left room for economic forgiveness that would not be tolerated in a less robust economic climate. Many of the recipients of the advice had neither the aptitude nor the desire to take into consideration more global events or circumstances. Considering these issues too far removed from their immediate reality, and readily being able to understand the advice or product they were being sold, was already enough of a challenge. Hence, the "dumbing down" of explanations served the purpose of being more marketable. Moreover, many of the financial sales people may not have been able to recognize, understand, and explain these implications of further global issues themselves. Unfortunately, being able to sell a product or offer advice which is more palatable for a client has little to do with how events unfold from the structural complexity upon which they are based, and their real impact on individual financial circumstances.

I have identified seven global areas I believe to be of immense importance in their impact of our future personal financial lives. My intent is to discuss and explain these events and their potential impacts in a way that will make them accessible by anyone with an open mind willing to make a reasonable effort to inform themselves.

The concept of thrift was one of the core values upon which the United States was founded, as embodied in a statement attributed to Benjamin Franklin, "A penny saved is a penny earned." Unfortunately, core values become watered down over successive generations until they become mere mythical cultural vestiges. They are relics having little relevance or bearing upon the behavior and decision making of the contemporary population.

Until four to five years ago, it was a quite illuminating to contrast the difference in financial perspectives between people of different generations. Older individuals, who had experienced the Great Depression in the early Twentieth Century, were much more frugal in their choices of expenditures. These were the parents of the baby boomers. In recent years I have noticed that the frugal and cautious nature of the Great Depression survivors appears to be succumbing to the pressures of consumption. Maybe their resistance has been worn down. Perhaps they realize they are approaching the end of their days and believe they have sufficient financial resources to carry them through their remaining lives.

Retiring in Red is part of a series of briefing papers which documents debt among subgroups of the U.S. population and looks at the growth of debt among older Americans. The results of the research are alarming. Looking at Americans over age 65, the number of these older Americans filing for bankruptcy tripled between 1992 and 2001. This makes them the fastest growing age group entering bankruptcy court. Credit card debt appears to be what is driving these seniors into bankruptcy. The key findings from this briefing during the period covered by this study, 1992-2001 were:

- Average self-reported credit card debt among seniors increased by 89%.
- Seniors between the ages of 65 and 69 had the most rapid rise in credit card debt of 217%.
- Among seniors with annual incomes under $50,000, representing 70% of seniors, one in five families spent over 40% of their income on debt repayments.

A common misconception is that this age group represents a relatively well-off segment of the American population. The facts suggest otherwise. Nearly 40% of these seniors are classified as "low-income" or below. Rising costs for housing, healthcare, and energy combined with low income and declining retirement wealth paint disturbing pictures for these individuals and America, indicating that seniors and the elderly are financially poorly prepared for their retirement years. If America is committed to having a social safety net for the most vulnerable of its population, we can expect increasing governmental budgetary costs for assisting the growing population of needy elderly at a time when government deficit growth is already out of control. A sober assessment of these circumstances portrays a rather compelling case for questioning the future solvency of America.

Tens of millions of Americans are what is known as the baby boomers. The majority of these baby boomers are prospective future retires and seniors in the 55-64 age groups. My general observation of and experience with the baby boomers is that they will not have a level of retirement income, nor the resources, to meet their expenditure levels. This observation is supported in the findings of the <u>Retirement in Red</u> briefing paper. Some of the findings with regard to this age group are as follows:

- 14% of 64 year olds are facing retirement with negative net worth.
- Nearly one out of every two families headed by someone between 47 and 64 years of age will be unable to replace at least half their income after retirement.
- Between 1989 and 1998 there was a decline in the home equity of these same families as more borrowed against their homes, often to pay off higher-interest credit card debt.
- Health care costs are a major concern of this group.

While these figures are disconcerting enough, more recent data suggests that the financial preparedness of these Americans has deteriorated further from the time period covered by the <u>Retiring in Red</u> report.

Alan Greenspan was the chairman of the Federal Reserve Bank of the United States. The Federal Reserve Bank is the central bank of the United States and is responsible for monitoring the economy and establishing monetary policy for a smoother running economy. One would expect that Chairman Greenspan would have had access to some of the best economic data. He should have a pretty good sense of the pulse of the economy. In his testimony before the Senate on February 16, 2005, Chairman Greenspan noted that the personal savings rate in the United States had dropped to an average of only 1% during 2004. Over the previous three decades the personal savings rate in the United States had averaged nearly 7% per year.

The personal savings rate is a measure of how much individual Americans are saving for their future needs. Viewing this portrays a picture of low and decreasing levels of personal savings rate combined with high and increasing levels of personal debt.

This is a recipe for national insolvency. At a time when the average American is in the financial hole, especially with respect to future retirement needs, rather than digging out of it, they are digging deeper into it. In fact, the recent real estate boom from about 2002-through 2005 created such an exaggerated notion of financial well-being for many people that their home became sophisticated ATM's used to cash out their equity to finance current consumption. Unfortunately, the time to pay the piper is resulting in increasing numbers of homes heading into the foreclosure process. Are we looking at a new generation of formerly solid middle-class Americans who are aging, homeless, and impoverished? Time will tell, and probably not too distantly in the future.

There are families and individuals that have developed financially responsible behaviors. They have accumulated nice-size nest eggs and appear to be sitting in a comfortable position. If you are among this group, you are to be commended for your financial foresight, discipline, and perhaps some luck, in the management of your financial affairs.

However, the problem is that is that even if we have done well and acted responsibly as individuals, we are members of a society. For better or for worse, the overall financial health of the society affects each member of that society.

The observable consequence resulting from watering down the value of thrift is that consumption has become a pathological behavior as it evolves into the addiction of over-consumption. It is pathological in that the level of consumer expenditure rises to the point of constantly increasing indebtedness. This has lead to the financial leveraging of the personal financial future of individuals and families, the result of which will be insolvency.

A preview of this can be seen in the current and increasing level of personal and business bankruptcies and foreclosures. A recent article in the *Wall Street Journal* reported that, according to the Federal Reserve, Americans owe $2.12 trillion, not including their mortgages, an increase of 110% over a decade ago. If assets and income had increased proportionately, this figure might not be so worrisome. However, financial assets increased only 94% and incomes increased only 65% during this same period. During 2004, 1.59 million people filed for bankruptcy, almost double the number of filings a decade earlier.1 While filing for bankruptcy has appeared to have lost the social stigma attributed to it in the recent past, governmental and institutional alarm is growing as documented by the passage of the 2005 bankruptcy legislation designed to thwart this avenue of escape.

At the same time that Americans are sinking deeper and deeper into debt, the population data portrays an aging population that will attempt to exit the workforce through retirement. However, a major segment of the population will be disappointed by their retirement prospects. Many others of the population will likely be in dire circumstances. They will have few financial resources with which to sustain themselves. At the same time they will likely have increased expenses arising from deteriorating health conditions and increased medical costs. The social safety net of Federal and State entitlement programs such as Social Security, Medicare, and Medicaid are becoming, and will become more so, frayed by increasing demand for these services. President Bush's Fiscal 2005 budget proposed a reduction of $1.5 billion in net federal funding for Medicaid and a reduction of nearly $16 billion over the 10-year period from 2005 through 2014. At the same time, a Kaiser Foundation report cites a need for the increased funding of Medicaid. Medicaid is revenue sharing program in which the Federal Government assists states in meeting the medical and health needs of the poor.

These events are taking place during a time in which the same social and cultural ethos that leads to individual over-indebtedness has been occurring at governmental levels as well. As our society has become more complex, the task of becoming well informed and rationally deliberative has become more and more onerous with the increasing complexity and number of issues, viewpoints, and agendas that emerge. The presumption of personal and social entitlement, in conjunction with a democratic system whose representatives depend upon the will of the people for their election, has resulted in staggering governmental fiscal and trade deficits.

For the last fifteen years I have had the opportunity and privilege to work with people planning their financial futures. Although one might expect that the starting point for this work would be with the facts and figures that represent the numerical summation of a person's life, I have found the reality to be that the hopes, dreams, and fears that people bring to the table is the underlying starting point in planning for the future. These hopes, dreams, and fears have been shaped by what a person has come to believe and value, and the experiences they have had. What I have also experienced, however, is that many of these hopes, dreams, and fears change as a person's experiences and circumstances change. What seems to be very important at one stage of life may have little significance at another stage. It may also be true that what seems to have little importance at one stage of life may have great significance at another stage. For example, if a person is lucky enough to be earning a good income, purchasing decisions and the assumption of debt do not have the same significance as these decisions do if one loses one's job, retires, or experiences an adverse financial event such as an illness, disability, or divorce. Despite the prevalence of these types of events occurring, as a general rule people do not adequately prepare for these events. Inadequate preparation for these contingencies takes difficult life events and transforms them into personally devastating events. The result is added stress to personal relationships, destruction of marriages, stress-related health conditions, and added entitlement costs to society which must somehow reintegrate these damaged lives into a care system.

One of the objectives of good financial planning is to try to strike a balance between what is, or appears to be, important today and what will be important in the future. A fundamental assumption upon which economics is based is that we live in a world in which there are limited resources, such as time, money, or energy. The reality of having an income that is limited is driven home when it becomes time to pay for our housing, gas, food, or any of the other innumerable things we need and want in our lives. Good personal financial decisions involve tradeoffs between enjoying ourselves today and what we may need or wish to enjoy tomorrow. Too many people make dysfunctional financial decisions, but not because they lack intelligence or the ability to make better decisions. Many of these poor financial decisions are being made by bright and motivated people who are successful in many other areas of their lives.

As an example, a woman, a single mother I once worked with, is a Ph.D. clinical psychologist with her own practice. For whatever reason, she decided having health insurance was not a high priority. At my advice she acquiesced and got herself and daughter health insurance. As she did not really believe she needed it, she had no sense of urgency in getting her application filled out and submitted. In the interim, while the application was aging on her desk, she awoke one morning with intense abdominal pain and required an emergency room visit, surgery, and hospitalization. Two months later, she had accumulated over $250,000 of uninsured medical bills. She was also not able to work in the interim. She was self-employed with no disability insurance and minimal savings. Her financial circumstances deteriorated rapidly. I ran into her several years later. She had just declared bankruptcy and was in the process of selling her house and moving into a rental. Clearly, she was a capable and intelligent woman. However, her belief system about financial issues took an adverse financial event and transformed it into a devastating financial episode in her life. It will take many years for her to recover, if at all. Unfortunately, although the specifics change according to the uniqueness of personal circumstance, this general pattern is all too common.

In providing professional guidance, it is not my professional role to decide if a person's financial goals are right or wrong. By asking clarifying questions I may help illuminate consequences of choices, and a person may discover whether their chosen goals really are what they want. Once goals have been established, I can realistically evaluate how attainable they might be and chart a course to increase the probability of their attainment.

One of the benefits of observing and participating in the financial planning and decision making of people in varied circumstances is the development of a professional perspective. It has been immensely interesting and insightful to observe people close in age with similar amounts of money, comparable intelligence and education, as they make financial choices with vastly different outcomes.

One of the most revealing circumstances of the differing outcomes of financial decision making is when a relatively large windfall, such as inheritance, is received. My own direct observation is that people generally make fairly poor choices that result in financial outcomes that significantly compromise what could have been relatively secure financial futures. An example is of a man in his mid-fifties who received an inheritance of $700,000 from his father. An intelligent man with moderate education, he was able bodied with no major health issues, but without a stable income earning capacity. He had managed to get by financially over the years, but had not really accumulated much in terms of a sound financial base. As with many people, relationship issues along with divorce and the raising of children had provided him his share of adverse life events. The inheritance was a sizable sum for this individual. If managed prudently, it could have provided him a modest, but financially relatively secure lifestyle, for the remainder of his life. However, this fellow also had his own set of dreams, one of which was to establish his own art studio to display his small collection of work. In his initial assessment of his circumstances he realized the opportunity for financial security his inheritance had brought him. In reconciling the objective between a lifetime of potential financial security and the risk of going for his dream, he decided that he would put at risk $50,000 of his new capital. Although this seemed like a reasonable plan in balancing these objectives, from a business point of view I do not believe he would have found an alternative source of financing with the sketchy business plan he had. At least, however, he had a plan that would limit his potential loss to something that might be manageable. Despite my concerns about his decision based upon many years of observation, experience, education, training, and participation in financial planning, investing, and financial decision making with small businesses and individuals, I cannot claim to have a crystal ball as to the certainty of future outcomes. There are many times when life does not go according to plan. There are also many times when people don't follow the plan they have. As it turned out, this fellow did not follow the plan he had. Six years later he had "invested" most of his inheritance in his dream and had yet to generate any regular or sustainable income from his venture.

Although this might seem like an extreme example of poor financial decision making, professional discussions with other financial advisors, CPA's, and attorneys have corroborated that my veteran experiences and observations are not unusual or unique. While the specific configuration of these decisions and circumstances vary widely, they share common denominators.

My observation is that the largest single common shared characteristic in people's financial decision making is that in many instances they do not make well thought-out, rational financial choices. The agenda's of people are complex and varied. Beliefs, desires, family and social pressures, psychological and emotional needs are huge factors in the financial decision making process. While these factors potentially add non-material richness, spirit, and meaning to our lives, they also responsible for much suffering, grief, and hardship that arise in the wake of the devastation caused by unwise choices.

I do not mean to imply that a rational planned financial strategy is a guarantee of a successful financial outcome. Real life is filled with too many uncontrollable variables and uncertainties for any kind of guaranteed outcomes. However, our personal financial circumstances are important to our well being, and we need to be motivated to try to shift the probability of successful financial outcomes in our favor. A systematic approach to clarifying one's goals, mapping out a strategy to reach those goals, and trying to identify what risks and obstacles might be encountered in trying to reach those goals provides a strategy that increases the probability of success. Unfortunately, even if this planning procedure were to be done well, it does not amount to much more than a conceptual intellectual exercise unless a person is able to internalize the reality of financial decision making cause and effect in bringing about desirable outcomes. Fortunately, this conviction need not be solely faith based. It can be facilitated by learning basic economic and financial principles. Once these basic principles are acquired, they provide a way of experiencing, observing, and thinking, which reinforces, expands, and deepens the understanding of our economic relationship with the world and the impact of events in that relationship. This is the foundation for effective personal financial decision making.

As a practical matter, however, I find an absence of rudimentary financial and economic understanding prevailing among the public. This observation applies across age, sex, education, and income levels. However, individuals with a higher net worth that has been accumulated by their own efforts seem to have a better grasp of financial and economic issues and/or tend to be more cognizant of the limitations of their knowledge. They are more willing to seek advice and to apply critical reasoning concerning the quality of advice they receive. This is an improvement over the general population's understanding and facility, perhaps allowing the accrual of more assets to these individuals. In a world where people make poor financial decisions, people who more wisely evaluate choices and outcomes will have a competitive advantage in achieving their objectives.

However, even the success of these individuals may be a result of regional thinking about economic and financial matters. For them, success has come by being in the right place at the right time. Regional thinking, which has its limitations, reflects responses to more immediate and localized concerns. In contrast, a more global type of thinking would also take into consideration issues and events that may be farther removed, thus impacting personal financial circumstances.

It is relatively easy to be dismissive and marginalize events which do not immediately impact one's world. Because of their magnitude, global issues provide the context within which the more immediate events in our lives occur. With regard to economic and financial issues, it is the die cast by the larger structural global issues that colors the immediacy of our personal agenda's and lives. It is the global economic and financial issues which set the scene for the events that play out in the local landscape. If greater awareness and understanding can be developed about which major global issues are the financial hurricanes that may be heading in our direction, then we can develop strategies concerning how we might best prepare for them. While this does not assure that we experience no impact from these events, it does increase the likelihood that we are better prepared to weather them.

I am not suggesting that everyone take up the study of finance and economics. Delving into the academic intricacies of these areas is a lifelong endeavor. It would not be a productive use of time and energy for most people. It is not necessary in order to develop an appreciation and feel for being able to recognize the geopolitical and economic clouds that warn of an impending serious storm. I believe that the missing link between these major geopolitical and economic storm clouds and developing an effective personal financial strategy is having an understanding of what the potential impact of these global events might be on a personal and localized level.

I have become increasingly alarmed about seven specific issues. They receive media coverage on a daily basis. The problem in fully recognizing their importance in our personal financial circumstances surfaces because they are part of the mainstream media coverage. What we hear tends to be fragmented and disconnected. There is lack of cohesiveness in integrating this information into a useful framework for personal financial decision making. This results in a diminished capacity for making effective financial decisions. Additionally, while these issues are frequently discussed by experts, they frequently neglect to consider them when discussing their analyses of current and future conditions. It is my intention to remedy these deficiencies by highlighting and discussing what I believe these issues to be. I will then consider their importance and potential implications at the level of personal financial decision making by showing the potential impact of these major political and economic events in our personal lives. My further intention is to create accessibility to these issues which results in a better understanding of their importance in our lives. Additionally, by presenting and discussing these issues within one context, I believe that recognition of the possibility that one or more of these events may occur at the same time will magnify the relevance of these issues in relationship to one another and to their potential impact in our lives. Despite the huge magnitude of financial hazard which may be unfolding before us, some people will emerge from it having done well. Within every experience, there are strategic opportunities. I will also present those areas of strategic opportunity which may allow one to emerge from the approaching financial storm intact and perhaps even more prosperous.

This book is intended to be a personal professional perspective and not an academic work. It is more a measure of the gleanings of my readings, observation, and experience over the last fifteen years. The reader will have to come to his or her own conclusion concerning the personal usefulness of my viewpoint in their future financial decision making. I recognize that all of the issues which I will discuss inevitably will have points of view associated with them which differ from my own. It is my hope that this work will at least serve as a foundation and stimulus for further thought as the reader comes to their own conclusions as to the importance and relevance of these issues in their own personal financial circumstances.

There are many serious problems in the world, and it is difficult to put them all into a manageable context that is useful in thinking about their potential impact and relevance to our personal lives. As I mentioned, I have identified seven areas which I believe to represent the core drivers of current and future economic conditions. Each of these areas represents a hazard which could destabilize the political and economic system of both the United States and the rest of the world. I believe there is a relationship between economic, political, social conditions, and the financial and investment markets. As a consequence, each of the seven areas I have identified represents a threat to your personal financial circumstances and well being. They are Seven Hazards to Your Financial Health. If one or more of these occur together or in close proximity to one another, they may create the Perfect Financial Storm. I believe this to be a real possibility, since the deterioration of events in any one of these areas is likely to trigger a deterioration of conditions in the others.

The Hazards to Your Financial Health are:

- The U.S. Twin Deficits—The Budget Deficit and the Trade Deficit
- Personal and Corporate Debt
- Pension Insolvencies
- Health Care Costs & Demographics
- Energy and Resource Limitations
- Corporate Malfeasance and Lapses of Ethical Conduct
- Geopolitical Events and Terrorism

I will cover each of these hazards in depth in the coming chapters. A brief preview of how and why these hazards may impact you is as follows:

The U.S. Twin Deficits—The Budget Deficit and the Trade Deficits

The Federal Budget Deficit is one measure of how much more the Federal government is spending than it is receiving in revenues. The official federal deficit is very large. In order to fund this deficit the federal government must borrow money. When it borrows money, it must pay interest on what it borrows just as any other borrower. The interest payments become an ongoing expense and add to the size of the ongoing deficit. Just as an individual can keep charging expenses on a credit card as long as there is someone willing to lend the money, this arrangement may continue for quite some time as long as there are willing lenders. Sooner or later lenders become less willing to lend as the borrower becomes more and more indebted. Lenders become concerned about the ability of the borrower to repay the loans. The more indebted the borrower, the more risk the lender has of the borrower defaulting. The lender may require increased compensation in the form of higher interest rates, or they may cease lending altogether if the perceived risk is too high, and if there are other more qualified borrowers.

In order for the United States to find sufficient funding for its budget deficit, it must seek draw upon overseas lenders. Currently, the United States needs to borrow $60 billion per month from overseas lenders in order to fund the budget deficit. Many of these are from central banks which are the foreign equivalent of the Federal Reserve Bank of the United States. They accumulate vast amounts of U.S. dollars because of the trade deficits. The trade deficit means that the United States buys much more from foreign countries than it sells to them. As a consequence, these foreign countries' U.S. dollar reserves grow. Since the U.S. is short on money, these dollars are loaned back to the United States. The willingness of these foreign lenders has allowed the United States to keep interest rates low. Low interest rates make money available for consumers to continue their purchases. A large percentage of these purchases originate from foreign sources. Low interest rates also make it easier to fund mortgages for home purchases and have helped fuel the appreciation in real estate prices. Hence, the United States has a vendor financing arrangement with other countries. The United States buys their goods and services and transfers U.S. dollars to these countries in exchange for these purchases. The countries then funds the U.S. dollars back to the United

States for a new cycle of purchasing and lending. All the while, the United States gets deeper in debt and poorer.

One of the hazards of this arrangement is that it has allowed the illusion of prosperity to continue in the United States, a mirage that could vanish quickly. If the foreign lenders decide they have loaned the United States enough money, their reluctance to continue loaning money to the United States could force interest rates up. Depending on how rapidly this event occurred, it could create a substantial economic shock in the United States. Increasing interest rates slow consumer purchases and put a damper on economic growth. At the same time, many loans which have variable interest rates would add additional costs to the already financially over committed consumer. This is the type of investment environment in which both stocks and bonds would, in general, do poorly.

Personal Debt

The U.S. consumer has been serving as the buyer of last resort in the domestic and world economic markets. In the United States, personal consumption is responsible for approximately two-thirds of economic growth and activity. The growing indebtedness and low savings rate of the American consumer suggest that this is not a sustainable financial picture. At some point credit cards and credit lines become tapped out. When this happens, we can expect decline in a recession or depression, an increase in personal and institutional insolvencies, and a shakeout of marginal successful businesses. At the same time over the last several years as the U.S. consumers balance sheet has been weakening, corporate balance sheets have become stronger as corporations have increased their cash positions. These are important considerations in investment planning for this type of environment, because they are factors which may have a significant impact on future investment results by their effect on the profitability and viability of different types of businesses.

Pension Insolvencies

The Pension Benefit Guaranty Corporation (PBGC) is a quasi-governmental organization set up to ensure that pensions of U.S. workers have some protection in the event the company sponsoring the plan becomes unable to honor its pension promise to its workers. Several years ago the PBGC was operating at a surplus of $8-$9 billion. However, due to the large pension plans for which PBGC has assumed responsibility over the last several years; the PBGC is now running at a deficit of approximately $25 billion. For example, United Airlines is one of the latest companies to have their pension plan assumed by the PBGC. In the event additional large pension plans are transferred to the PBGC, the U.S. government may be faced with the prospect of having to bailout the PBGC in order to continue to honor pension promises to U.S. workers, thereby placing an additional financial burden on the federal government at a time when the deficit is already huge. The impact on personal finances depends on how the government handles this additional financial demand. One possibility would be for the government to raise taxes, another to increase the premiums participating companies pay for being insured by the PBGC. A third would be to refuse to bail out the PBGC. I don't believe this last alternative is very likely because of the level of social and personal economic distress that would occur in the event the pensions were altogether lost by retirees. In any event, any of the alternatives chosen by the government to bail out the PBGC would probably have an overall negative impact on the investment environment and the personal economic circumstances of most Americans.

Health Care Costs & Demographics

Health insurance and health care costs have become a major variable of the well-being of America on personal, corporate, and governmental levels. From the costs of federal and state governments for entitlements such as Medicare and Medicaid, to the escalating expenses to corporations for employee benefit costs of current and retired employees, to the uninsured or underinsured individuals and families, the rapidly increasing cost of health care is compromising the already tenuous financial picture of the United States. Joined with the factors of the demographics as well as the general state of physical health with obesity as a regular mainstream media item, we can see how frayed the fabric of the United States social structure has become. I have observed individuals who have done an excellent job of saving and investing during their working life not able to take an early retirement because of the impact the loss of their health insurance benefits would have on their financial circumstances.

Energy and Resource Limitations

The concerns and implications about adequate energy supply availability have become mainstream issues impacting our lives. While there are many opinions regarding the severity of the issue, the fact is that there has been a stunning and rapid rate of appreciation of the price of oil. From an investment point of view, the economics of this area suggest the possibility of significant gains in future years with the financial and economic implications extending into every area of your life. Relatively inexpensive energy and oil are at the foundation of the way of life we have come to know. High prices and limited availability may represent a magnitude 9 financial earthquake to this way of life.

Corporate Malfeasance and Lapses of Ethical Conduct

When considering investment decisions, two primary factors determine the merit of the investment decision— what is the potential risk and what is the potential reward. In order for an investor to evaluate the risk and reward of a prospective investment, reliable information is needed about the opportunity. Full and fair disclosure of relevant information has been a cornerstone upon which the American system of capitalism was developed. Such information allows the investor to come to an informed conclusion about whether or not they are willing to accept the risks of a particular investment in exchange for potential return. Lapses of ethical conduct and corporate malfeasance involve some type of deception with the intent to create or maintain the perception that things are better than they really are. While these lapses of ethical conduct have always been a part of the business and investment environment, usually they were an occasional aberration that allowed a high enough level of investor confidence in an acceptable environment. However, in recent years we have witnessed some of the most sophisticated and devious looting that has ever occurred. The amount of wealth stolen and lost in these transactions has been enormous. Unfortunately, the level of complicity of these schemes involved the guardians of financial reporting, integrity, CPA's, agents of the court, and attorneys, as well as high-level political innuendo. This situation has the potential to erode the entire foundation of American capitalism. It undermines the confidence and belief of prospective investors who believe they have adequate and reliable information on which to base their investment decisions.

Geopolitical Events and Terrorism

Increasing globalization has transformed the world into a system of political and economic interdependencies. Technology has provided global access to information and ideas that is unprecedented in human history. Investment capital flows readily throughout the world and businesses can relocate or acquire resources in ways that offer opportunity for greater operational efficiency. On the surface it would seem that this would be an ideal set of circumstances for uplifting the global economic climate and promote prosperity and greater affluence throughout the planet. The reality, however, is quite different. The events of September 11, 2001, were a tragic and dramatic reminder that all is not well in Camelot. The grim reality of this event demonstrated that a handful of committed and zealous individuals could bring the world's greatest economic and military power to its knees armed with no more than their hearts, minds, and the lowest of technological apparatus.

With a new demand for economic and intellectual resources, the fight against terrorism represents a global guerilla war waged against organized institutions by an enemy that is decentralized. Israel, with decades of experience with this type of conflict, is an example of how long this type of conflict can continue within the confines of a small geographical and political boundary. The theatre of engagement in the war on terrorism is no longer confined to a specific geographical region. It is likely that the hundreds of billions of dollars already spent are just the beginning of a sustained and increasing demand for economic resources. In planning our personal financial futures, we need to ask ourselves what impact this reallocation of America's economic resources will have on the United States, and how we might best prepare to meet these challenges.

References
1. McGhee, Heatherand Draut, Tamara, Retiring in the Red, The Growth of Debt Among Older Americans, Borrowing to Make Ends Meet Briefing Paper #1, Second Edition, Demos, A Network for Ideas and Action.
2. http://www.demos-usa.org/pubs/borrowing_to_make_ends_meet.pdf.
3. Testimony of Chairman Greenspan, Federal Reserve Board's semiannual Monetary Report to the Congress Before the Committee on Banking, Housing, and Urban Affairs, U.S. Senate February 16, 2005.
4. Schroeder and Wang, Wall Street Journal, P. 1, Sweeping New Bankruptcy Law To Make Life Harder for Debtors, 4/6/2005.

CHAPTER TWO
The Twin Deficits & Governmental Mismanagement

W hen Hurricanes Katrina and Rita were heading to the Gulf of Mexico, people who were knowledgeable about these types of storms were able to predict with a relatively high degree of certainty the direction, the likely locations of impact, and the intensity of these natural disasters. Naturally, the closer these devastating storms came to the U.S. Gulf Coast, the easier it was to predict these things. Unfortunately, the closer these storms came to their destructive destinations, the more difficult it was to escape their impact. There were, however, credible predictions from reliable sources, far enough in advance that should have provided sufficient response time for a great many more people to have avoided some of the personal harm from the destructive force of these storms. Despite the potential for an early warning, the destruction arising from these hurricanes was far in excess of what could have been avoided. A combination of complacency, government ineptness, and a lack of individual resources resulted in amplifying the destruction and unavoidable damage.

Studying the response to these hurricanes illuminates how people perceive and respond to risks. For one thing, a Hurricane Katrina was a possible, but low probability, event. This means that the expected frequency of its occurrence was low enough not to be considered a realistic possibility in people's decision making. Even when the size and potential destructive force of this hurricane was confirmed, the recognition of the reality of its presence was delayed until the hurricane actually hit, and in many cases, not until it had come and gone.

For any particular problem or crisis, two broad strategic approaches of response exist. One would be to pursue a proactive course. The second would be a reactive response. Behavior falling into the first one of not dealing with serious issues until they arise impairs the ability to decrease the potential damage from harmful events. These same methods are also present in personal and institutional economic decisions. In this chapter we will look at the potential devastation from existing monumental global economic balances which have arisen along with the twin U.S. budget and trade deficits central to this story.

Moreover, we will examine the potential impact on personal financial circumstances, and we will explore potential opportunities or safe harbors from a possible impending Class 5 financial hurricane.

Bretton Woods

As with most social conditions, our current global economic environment has its roots in past events. The end of the First World War was followed by huge war reparation costs, inflation, and a global depression. These conditions set the scene for the Second World War, which also left in its wake a devastated global financial system. In an attempt to be proactive in reconstructing the a global economic system, and avoid some of the mistakes following the First World War, the United States convened an economic conference of the Allies to decide what the future economic and monetary order of the world would look like. A month after D-Day, in July of 1944, forty-four nations represented by 700 delegates met at the Mount Washington Hotel in Bretton Woods, New Hampshire. The agreement that arose from this conference was signed on July 22, 1944. It came to be known as the Bretton Woods Agreement. In addition to establishing the

International Monetary Fund and laying the groundwork for creating the Bank for International Settlements, the Agreement provided that most currencies of the world would be pegged to the U.S. dollar, so that a specific exchange relationship would exist between one currency and another. The dollar, in order to have a specified value would be valued relative to gold. The relationship was established to be $35 to one ounce of gold. Essentially, the Bretton Woods Agreement formally established gold to be the basis of a global currency value and to the dollar in particular.

The American currency system was originally set up to operate on a gold and silver exchange system. The Act that set up the system, in 1792, provided that anyone could bring gold or silver to the mint and have it rapidly coined into U.S. currency. This gold and silver currency system operated until 1933 when Teddy Roosevelt, responding to the stock market crash of 1933, signed an act designed to prohibit the hoarding of gold. By Executive order, U.S. citizens were no longer allowed to exchange dollars for gold, although other countries and foreign banks were allowed to continue to exchange their U.S. dollars for gold. Ownership of gold became nationalized, and it became illegal for an American citizen to hold gold coins or bullion in excess of nominal amounts. Within a period of three weeks, banks, financial institutions, and individuals were supposed to turn in gold coins, bullion, and gold certificates. The reason for Roosevelt's concern was that, following the stock market crash of 1929, Americans had lost faith in American currency and its financial institutions. There were runs on banks where depositors wanted to exchange their paper money for gold. This presented Roosevelt with a problem because his interest was in trying to stimulate the economy. Since the U.S. currency system was based upon the reserves of gold it held, a decrease in these gold reserves by citizens cashing in dollars for gold meant that the ability of the Federal Government to borrow money to finance economic and social programs was limited and in jeopardy.

We can see from this that linking a currency system to gold or silver exchange can place a limit on what might be responsible governmental policy-making ability in response to a national crisis. The other side of the story, however, is that by requiring the government to have some type of monetary conversion of paper money to a clearly identifiable and readily ascertainable standard of measuring value, government is prevented from overspending and over-borrowing to meet what might be politically expedient expenditures. This leaves the present and future citizens of this country having to pay tomorrow for the indulgencies of the present day. While we may view democracy as the greatest governing system to emerge in history, the unfortunate truth is that it is not without its weaknesses. The nature of winning and maintaining political office is what can be promised and delivered to voter constituencies. Promises have to be paid for in some way. Money has to be available to make these payments. If the amount of money available is limited by such things as the amount of gold that is available to back up these promises to pay, obstacles to the political process occur.

While mandating a conversion ratio between gold and the dollar, the Bretton Woods Agreement acknowledged the need for a definable standard of monetary discipline, but it proved itself to be too politically cumbersome to the aspirations of governing politicians. Only a fraction of bank deposits are regularly held by the bank with the remaining deposits loaned to other customers. This is called a fractional reserve type of banking system.

Similarly, with dollar to gold convertibility, by setting a fixed dollar/gold conversion ratio the supply of U.S. dollars is theoretically limited by the amount of gold available to back it up. High redemptions of dollars in exchange for gold were not originally expected. By the mid 1960's the costs of the Vietnam War and social spending programs had contributed to increasingly large U.S. budget deficits and dollar supply. Resulting inflationary pressures had pushed up the market price of gold above the $35 per ounce official price, meaning that the U.S. government was obligated to sell gold at $35 per ounce to market participants, including foreign central banks. By 1971, all the play that could be extracted from this asset-based monetary system had been played. President Richard Nixon suspended the convertibility of the dollar into gold on August 15, 1971. At this juncture in American economic history, the U.S. government transformed the U.S. dollar into a fiat currency. Its value was not backed by anything other than faith. Gold notes and silver certificate dollars were replaced with Federal Reserve Notes, and the phrase "Payable to the Bearer Upon Demand" was replaced with "In God We Trust".

To paraphrase an old saying, *Trust in God, but remember to tie up your horses.*

While faith in the value of the U.S. dollar may have been an admirable testimonial to the global belief in America's economic strength, it also gave the government a blank check. Thereafter, each U.S. government administration pursued its political agendas without the discipline of adhering to realistic economic constraints, such as having to pay for what it was promising.

According to the historical data series compiled by the Congressional Budget Office, following the termination of the gold-backed dollar, the U.S. began running persistently high budget deficits, with the exception of the years 1968-2001. Running a budget deficit is no different for the government than it is for me, you, or for a business. It means that there are more expenses than income to pay for them. While there are circumstances that make a temporary budget deficit a reasonable and functional event, persistent and growing budget deficits are a sign of poor financial health and are dysfunctional. A budget deficit means that funds have to be borrowed from somewhere or someone. Lenders expect some form of payment for their services, usually in the form of interest payments on the money loaned. The rate of interest is expected to compensate the lender for being deprived of an alternative use of their funds as well as for assuming the risk that the borrower may default on their obligations to repay. Anyone who has had the experience of shopping for a mortgage or a credit card has probably experienced a difference in the interest rate offered depending on the credit rating of the borrower. The same financial principles apply to individuals, businesses, and governments. The U.S. government is an exception to this basic financial principle for two reasons—its unique ability to create money, and its role as a global reserve currency. This is especially true when there is no constraint, such as converting created money into a specified amount of gold. These unique characteristics have provided the United States with the ability to have low interest rates and very large budget deficits. Low interest rates are usually associated with contributing to economic expansion. Low interest rates encourage individuals and businesses to borrow for consumption and/or investment reasons. Borrowing for consumption means that businesses need to produce more products, expand their operations for additional production capacity, and hire more workers. Borrowing for investment means additional dollars chasing investments bid up in price by this process. While these things may seem as if they are good and may be a politically strong story for incumbent politicians, as the saying goes, "There is no free lunch."

A closer look at what is represented by professional spin doctors as healthy economic growth reveals the fragility of our current economic conditions, domestically, institutionally, and governmentally. We have seen how the Federal government has been running increasing budget deficits. In order to fund them, the government must borrow money from the public and from other programs within the government such as the Social Security Trust Fund. As of November 2005, the total amount of debt the Federal government owed was over $8 trillion. Nearly $4.6 trillion was debt held by the public, and about $3.4 trillion was debt held by other agencies of the government such as the Social Security Trust Fund. As of the fiscal year end of 2005, the interest alone on this debt was over $352 billion. According to the CIA World Factbook, the population of the U.S. as of July 2005 was just under 300 million people. To gain some perspective on the significance of the size of the Federal debt and its interest expense, a quick calculation of the approximately $8 trillion Federal debt and its $352 billion per year interest expense divided by the 300 million person population of the United States shows that the average Federal debt per man, woman, and child in the U.S. is $26,666. With the U.S. Census Bureau's estimate of the median earned income of Americans in 2004 being a bit over $44,000 per year, one has to become concerned about where the revenue is going to come from to pay for the interest on the Federal debt, let alone to pay down the debt.

Indeed, there is global concern about the deteriorating financial picture of the United States. The IMF, an international organization of 184 member countries, was established to promote international monetary cooperation, exchange stability, and orderly exchange arrangements; to foster economic growth and high levels of employment; and to provide temporary financial assistance to countries to help ease balance of payments adjustment. In a recent report the IMF concluded that:

"Although fiscal policies have undoubtedly provided valuable support to the recovery so far, the return to large deficits raises two interrelated concerns. First, with budget projections showing large federal fiscal deficits over the next decade, the recent emphasis on cutting taxes, boosting defense and security outlays, and spurring an economic recovery may come at the eventual cost of upward pressure on interest rates, a crowding out of private investment, and an erosion of longer-term U.S. productivity growth.

Second, the evaporation of fiscal surpluses has left the budget even less well prepared to cope with the retirement of the baby boom generation, which will begin later this decade and place massive pressure on the Social Security and Medicare systems. Without the cushion provided by earlier surpluses, there is less time to address these programs' underlying insolvency before government deficits and debt begins to increase unsustainably, making more urgent the need for meaningful reform."(January 7, 2004).

In this same report, when the IMF considered unfunded liabilities of the U.S. government, such as Social Security and Medicare benefits, the more realistic estimate of U.S. indebtedness may be as high as $47 trillion. A fiscally responsible U.S. policy would require an immediate and permanent 60 percent hike in the federal income tax yield, or a 50 percent cut in Social Security and Medicare benefits. Other institutions have come up with estimates ranging from

$21 trillion to the Social Security and Medicare trustees March 2004 estimate of $74 trillion. As Pete Peterson, a former U.S Secretary of Commerce, and founding member of the Concord Coalition points out in his book <u>Running on Empty</u>, "the reputations of these institutions run from conservative to liberal to bureaucratic, there can be nothing partisan about the basic message-".

The primary source of revenues for the Federal government is taxes. There are two ways in which the Federal debt can be managed. One way is to control Federal expenditures, which could prevent the debt from getting larger, and possibly pay down the existing debt. If the past history of the Federal government's fiscal behavior is any guide to the likelihood of this occurring, we are not offered much hope in this regard. In addition we have the ongoing costs of a global war on terrorism against a decentralized enemy who can emerge from no where and disappear into nowhere at a time and place of their choosing. W also have increased expenditures for entitlement spending as baby boomers age, and increased costs of interest payments from increasing government indebtedness and higher interest rates. Also, there are the costs of unknown and off budget contingency events such as funding for natural disaster relief, or possibly having to bail out the Pension Benefit Guarantee Corporation in the event their assumed liabilities become more than they can handle, or keeping whole a major financial institution in the case of a Long Term Capital Management type occurring, such as a financial derivative debacle. Long Term Capital Management was a large hedge fund that in September, 1998, had such large losses it was on the brink of failure. They had so many large institutional type investors, that the Federal Reserve Bank became concerned that their failure would have dire financial consequences for global financial markets. The Federal Reserve Bank organized a rescue for Long Term Capital Management to prevent this from occurring. The failure of a major financial institution would have consequences that would go well beyond this. The problem with living beyond one's means is that the proverbial "rainy day fund" does not exist.

Solving this Federal Budget problem by eliminating the annual deficit through control on expenditures does not seem likely. If we look at the Federal Budget 2006 chart on spending, and consider the Health, Social Security, Income Security, and Defense categories, we can see they comprise over 80% of Federal expenditures. Cutting these areas would have significant social and political consequences. The Congressional Budget Office, who by their own analysis considers their budget forecasts to be optimistic, sees continuing deficits at least through the year 2015.

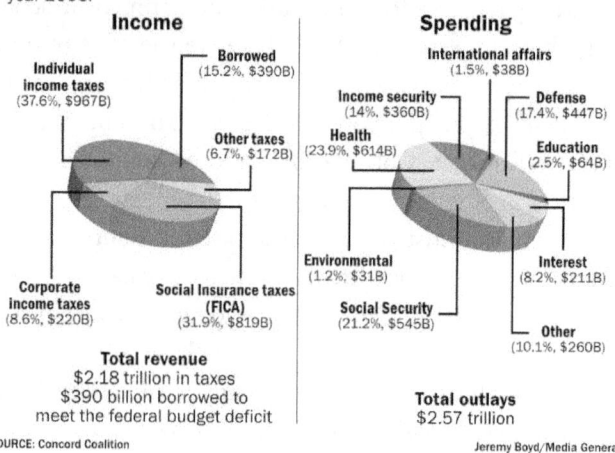

Federal budget 2006

Below is a breakdown of Federal Government income and spending for fiscal year 2006.

Income

Individual income taxes (37.6%, $967B)

Borrowed (15.2%, $390B)

Other taxes (6.7%, $172B)

Corporate income taxes (8.6%, $220B)

Social Insurance taxes (FICA) (31.9%, $819B)

Total revenue
$2.18 trillion in taxes
$390 billion borrowed to meet the federal budget deficit

Spending

International affairs (1.5%, $38B)

Income security (14%, $360B)

Health (23.9%, $614B)

Defense (17.4%, $447B)

Education (2.5%, $64B)

Environmental (1.2%, $31B)

Social Security (21.2%, $545B)

Interest (8.2%, $211B)

Other (10.1%, $260B)

Total outlays
$2.57 trillion

SOURCE: Concord Coalition

Jeremy Boyd/Media General

Federal revenues can be increased though taxes if economic growth is very strong and the taxes on these earnings make a significant contribution to Federal tax revenues to offset Federal spending. Another way Federal revenues could increase would be for the government to implement higher tax rates. Alternatively, some combination of these two outcomes could occur. The likelihood of this coming to pass does not appear great to me. Congressional Budget Office economic projections actually show the measure of economic growth, real GDP, decreasing through 2015. This would preclude increased tax revenues from an expanding economic base. It would be politically and economically difficult to make a case for increased taxes in the face of slow economic growth. From a budgetary point of view, it appears that the United States is financially between a rock and a hard spot.

Moreover, as interest rates increase, the interest expense of the government will also increase in the absence of meaningful debt reduction. How much Federal debt reduction, let alone meaningful debt reduction, would seem to be a bit of a quandary. As long as the Federal government runs a budget deficit, the Federal debt will grow. The Government must borrow money to keep operating. Even if the Government manages to balance the annual budget, it must still deal with the existing debt, and the unfunded liabilities which add to the burden. If we take a mid-range estimate of this indebtedness of $47 trillion, the International Monetary Fund's estimate, that works out to over $150,000 per man, woman, and child in the United States. Despite the smokescreens of talking heads and the pundits' assurances of the strength of the U.S. economy, the monumentally staggering, and growing, amount of Federal budget deficits and debt cannot be objectively viewed as anything other than a sign of the fragile economic foundation upon which the United States currently sits. In fact, calling these circumstances fragile is a generously optimistic description.

In the context of this huge amount of debt, reasonable questions to ask are who is loaning all this money to the Federal government, and what would happen if they decided to stop, decrease, or even disinvest from U.S. debt? One way to determine this is to look at who the current lenders are. According to the U.S. Treasury's September 2005 Treasury Bulletin, the two largest increases in lenders between March of 1994 and March of 2005 were the Federal Government and its agencies, and foreign sources. In the case of the Federal government borrowing from itself, or a closely related entity such as the Social Security trust fund, this appears to me to be an accounting sleight of hand similar to an Enron type off balance sheet tryst. Although the borrowing may not immediately show up as additional public indebtedness, the people with final responsibility for repayment of these borrowed funds will be the American public.

The other source of funds for U.S. government borrowing, foreign sources, is also very problematic. We have up to this point been discussing the U.S. budget deficit. A common term used to refer to the two colossal economic imbalances in the world is twin deficits. Similar to the September 11, 2001, destruction of the twin towers in New York City that represented a man made tragic disaster, the twin deficits may be viewed as twin towers of the global financial system. They represent man-made events that have the potential to be tragic economic disasters whose consequences will seriously impact the financial lives of the people of the world's economy.

The U.S. budget deficit is one of these twin towers. The other twin tower is what is referred to as the trade deficit, which means that more products and services are imported than are exported. When we are importing more than we are exporting, we have to pay for the foreign goods and services that we are purchasing. Another way to look at this is that as an exchange system we are exchanging dollars for foreign goods. We import foreign goods and services and we export dollars. The exporting of dollars represents a transfer of wealth to the countries producing what the U.S. is buying. No matter how affluent a country is, massive transference of its wealth, such as in the United States, will leave it less affluent. If a country still wishes or needs to continue its consumption behaviors, it will have to find a lender from which to borrow to continue its purchases. If the buyer also happens to be the biggest customer of the seller, the seller will find it in his interest to loan additional funds to the buyer to allow it to continue buying. This is called vendor financing, which is not an economic arrangement that can continue indefinitely. The longer it does continue, the larger the indebtedness of the borrower will become. The larger the indebtedness of the borrower is, the greater the risk to the lender. As with all economic arrangements, there is a tradeoff between the costs and the benefits of the economic arrangement. When the point arrives where the risks of continued lending to an already heavily indebted borrower begin to outweigh the benefits, the lender will seek to modify the terms of the arrangement.

In the case of the United States, exporting countries have been loaning money to us, a practice which has allowed the U.S. economy to maintain low interest rates. This availability of funding has enabled United States' consumers, already too heavily indebted, to continue the high consumption of imports. This supply low interest rate money has also contributed to an inflation of asset values in the real estate and stock markets by giving investors the wherewithal to bid up the prices of these assets. The bidding up of these asset values has, in turn, allowed them to be used as leverage for additional consumption of exports and provided investment capital for the continued bidding up of the real estate and stock markets.

The benefit to the exporting countries, who are loaning the U.S. money by buying its Treasury debt, is that the money they earn by the exporting of its goods and services to the U.S. has provided capital for further economic development in these countries. On the surface of it this might seem like a fairytale type story where everybody lives happily ever after in unbounded affluence until we remember the staggering debt load being accumulated by the United States. Moreover, economic globalization, which has made available less expensive consumer goods, has done this by opening up access to lower costs centers of production than the United States. The standard of, and cost of living in, the United States had made it uncompetitive as a manufacturing country, but it is now heading in that direction because of the shift of jobs and production capacity to outside the United States. However, at the same time the economy faces increasing governmental indebtedness, social needs, energy and defense costs, and rising costs of healthcare.

While public policy prescriptions address these issues, our purpose in this work is much more modest. Saving the world, and the United States for that matter, are both worthy endeavors. However, we do not feel up to this task. We are concerned with how one might position one's personal life and finances to avoid the hazards that may lie ahead, and ideally capitalize on prospective opportunities that present themselves in a perilous economic landscape. If, after giving a sober assessment to the preceding analysis, one concludes that a relatively accurate representation has been made of the U.S. and global economic picture, it would be imperative to one's current and future financial health to explore what the risks might look like and where the potential opportunities may be. It is in this vein that we offer the following for consideration.

There is general recognition and acceptance of the role interest rates play in stimulating or slowing the economy. This may be seen by observing the policies of the U.S. Central Bank, The Federal Reserve Bank. One of the roles of the Federal Reserve Bank is to assist the U.S. economy in maintaining an orderly and consistent rate of growth. Ideally, moderate rates of steady growth, unemployment at levels that are economically and politically acceptable and low inflation have been policy objectives.

The Federal Reserve Bank has several tools at its disposal and influences interest rates in the economy. When economic growth starts slowing beyond economic and political policy acceptable levels, it attempts to lower interest rates. Conversely, when economic growth is quick and increasing inflation becomes more of a concern, the Federal Reserve Bank will try using its tools to increase interest rates. It is important to recognize that the Federal Reserve Bank can attempt to influence interest rates, but it cannot mandate them. Ultimately, financial markets determine what the interest rates will be.

Interest rates are not different than other types of goods or services. An interest rate can be viewed as the price of renting money for a period of time. As with other prices, supply and demand are the market forces which affect price. If something, such as money, is in short supply and relatively high demand, a higher price can be charged for it. In the case of money, that means a higher interest rate which means that the power to influence interest rates depends upon how much control a banker has over the supply of money. A country's central banker, such as the Federal Reserve Bank, has traditionally been the primary source that controls the availability of money. However, that is no longer the case. Economic globalization and money outflows to foreign countries from which we import goods and services have allowed huge accumulations of U.S. dollars by other countries. At the same time, growing indebtedness has made the United States dependent on the grace, or other agendas, of these countries to loan money back. In effect, the new role of foreign countries has been to assume the role of a banker with the ability to significantly influence interest rates in the United States. Since interest rates play a central role in stimulating or slowing the economy, the dependence of the United States upon foreign infusions of money has transferred a great deal of economic control over the U.S. to the agenda of other countries, as well as foreign private interests. For example, whether for the economically sound reason of financial diversification, or the pragmatic reasons of establishing leverage for a specific set of political issues, a country or private interest decided not to continue loaning money to the U.S., interest rates in the U.S. would rise.

China would represent a good current example of this possibility. It is accumulating huge U.S. dollar reserves because of the large number of goods it exports to the U.S. It has been very pragmatic about reinvesting these dollars into the U.S. by purchasing Treasury debt. This has helped keep interest rates down and allowed consumers to pay for their purchasing preferences on easily available credit. As U.S. indebtedness increases and China develops other external and well as internal markets for its products, it will likely become reluctant to continue to fund the U.S. budget deficit without limit. Several countries, such as South Korea, have already expressed their concerns and desire to diversify away from funding the U.S. budget deficit to the extent they have been. Since the U.S. needs $60 billion per month of foreign capital to fund its budget deficit, higher interest rates would be required to reward investors willing to take the financial risk and forego other opportunities with their investment dollars.

The situation is the same with those countries accumulating huge reserves of petrodollars from the ravenous energy needs of the U.S. In this case, however, many of these countries happen to be Islamic countries with populations having unfavorable attitudes to the U.S. and with politically unstable circumstances themselves.

If this were to happen, it would lead to an economic slowdown in the U.S., which in turn would result in higher unemployment, which would fuel a further economic slowdown because of a decreased financial capacity to continue preferred levels consumption. We would also be likely to see an increase in financial insolvency and high rates of home foreclosures among individuals who could no longer afford to service their existing debt load. Businesses which were marginally profitable would fold amid increasingly competitive business conditions. This would further open up the door to increased imports from countries more competitive than the United States. In the past, these types of economic threats have contributed to isolationist and protectionist sentiments. There is no reason to believe that people would respond any differently nowadays. Were these circumstances to occur, they would result in greater political discord and polarization among countries.

This possible set of conditions, while painful, is a normal economic response to correct economic excesses. Economic recession is a process that culls economic inefficiency from the system and sets the foundation for healthy economic growth afterwards. It often results in downward pressure on the prices of goods and services because of increased competition.

However, some circumstances are accompanied by an increase in prices. This has occurred before and is known as stagflation, the worst of economic conditions. Rising prices at a time of diminished capacity for paying for them is the most socially painful and disruptive economic condition. There is reason to believe that we may be looking at just such an impending economic circumstance. High personal indebtedness of individuals and federal and state governments, sluggish employment opportunities, and an increasingly more competitive global business environment make a likely case for an economic slowdown.

At the same time, an increased demand for basic resources such as concrete, copper, timber, oil, and other energy sources are appearing from the rapidly emerging economies of the world. As economic development continues, this trend is likely to increase and be followed by an increased demand for the food produced globally. While one might believe that this growth would be good for the U.S. economy, one must remember that there are other countries in the world with which the U.S. must compete to supply these goods as well as compete to purchase them in an open market. In particular, China with its huge population, has taken its place at the table of demand for the world's resources. South America and Canada, resource rich countries, have been developing trade relationships with China that will benefit the economies of China and these other countries at the expense of U.S. interests. India is emerging right behind China as a heavyweight in the global economy. It will also be sitting at the table of the demand for the world's material and energy resources to fuel its rapid growth and will be a major competitor for the U.S. with its large population of well educated, industrious, technologically proficient, and relatively inexpensive workforce, especially in the services sector.

On the whole, the U.S. has gotten itself into the polarized position of being unfavorably viewed by much of the world's population. Increased demand for resources from these rapidly developing countries is likely to push up prices for these goods. This is especially true if the supply of these resources is limited, as numerous credible and knowledgeable commentators have noted about oil supplies. Increasing personal and governmental indebtedness and ever-increasing and larger value bankruptcy filings are signs of the poor financial health of the private sector. An economic expansion that is built upon ever increasing consumption, debt, and dis-saving is not indefinitely sustainable. While the image of affluence may be temporarily viable by this sort of economic regime, the underlying truth of the increasing impoverishment of the borrower will emerge as the burden of increasing debt becomes too much to bear.

Of immediate concern to the U.S. is how we might reduce or avoid our exposure to the economic hazards that may lie ahead. Ideally, we would like not only to avoid these future potential eventualities, we would like to identify where the opportunities may be. If our preceding analysis has merit, we may be looking at a future slow growth economic environment in the U.S. This would suggest that investing in U.S. stocks for growth, in general, would not offer the most promising opportunities. It appears likely that interest rates and inflation will both be increasing. If so, investing in bonds, whose value moves in the opposite direction as interest rates, would be a recipe for losing money. In addition, if business conditions worsen, because of a poor economy, we may be looking increasing credit quality deterioration in existing bonds. This also would decrease the value of bonds, especially longer term bonds. While financial institutions such as banks, insurance companies, and brokerages have done well in the recent past, at least a good part of the reason was being able to capitalize on low interest rates to increase their profitability margin in lending. An increase in interest rates and insolvencies may decrease their earning capacity. Assuming a real economic link between a company's business performance and its stick price, a decreased earning should result in a stagnant, if not decreased stock price. Financial institutions would not, therefore, look to offer promising prospects. Higher interest rates would also depress the currently overheated real estate sector and the associated supporting businesses, including home builders, many REITS, especially heavily leveraged ones, mortgage lenders, home furnishings, and appliance manufacturers. These areas would also appear to be good areas to avoid. Many of these sectors represent stalwart areas that have served as pillars in many traditional investment strategies. In the heyday of America's ascent to economic prominence these were good solid growth prospects. Failure to recognize the changing economic realities of the world by viewing these old line investments as they were in the past is likely to be the path to dashed expectations and financial distress.

When considering future financial risks and opportunities, a belief held by most people is that money plays a central role, which may not be true with respect to what is most generally assumed about money. One of the functions of money is to serve as a store of value. The most enduring historical basis of money was to be linked to a tangible asset, such as gold or silver. Money was a symbolic representation of a claim to a specific amount of a valued real asset. When governments departed from this basic principle, history suggests that political imperatives took precedence over sound economic policy and have resulted in the collapse of monetary systems that unlinked their money to a specific relationship to a real asset. Recall that the U.S. dollar is no longer backed by any real asset. This is what is known as a fiat currency. It has value only because the government declares that is has value, and as long as people accept the government's declaration. If history, economic, and political behaviors are to serve as any guides, we would reasonably expect that the dollar, as well as the other fiat currencies of the world, will experience a crisis of confidence. Richard Duncan, in his recent well researched and documented book, <u>The Dollar Crisis, Causes and Consequences</u>, offers an excellent analysis of this subject, although his proposed remedies do not appear to me to be realistic nor feasible.

A loss of confidence in government's economic policies, specifically the U.S., would undermine the value these currencies and result in people seeking other means with which to store the value of any accumulated wealth. It is likely that the historical function of gold and silver will again reemerge as a universally accepted store of value. Additionally, one might reasonably expect that since claims to real assets have served as true representations of wealth, assets which have a definable place in the global supply and demand system will again be favorably viewed as means with which to store value. Assets which represent a strategic significance to a country's well being would stand out as being of particular importance. Claims to energy related resources and their associated supporting industries would be a prime example. Natural resources needed by the rapidly growing economies of China and India might be other good examples.

Summary

In this chapter we have looked at a brewing storm of immense significance to the health of the global economic and financial system. The growing twin deficits of the United States, the budget deficit, and the trade deficit, represent a clear and present danger to your financial futures. They are to the point where it appears unlikely that any meaningful proactive remedy will emerge to correct the monumental global economic imbalances which exist. As a result, it is likely that financial assets whose value is based upon the assumed values supported by government declarations of value will suffer. These assets include bonds, financial institutions, marginal businesses, overly indebted businesses and governments, and leveraged real estate. Assets which may benefit as a result of these economic circumstances include assets that have historically served as representations of wealth, such as gold and silver. In addition, real assets, especially those that are of strategic significance to a country's well-being, are likely to benefit. These include energy related resources and their associated industries, as well as natural resources needed by countries experiencing high rates of economic growth, such as China and India.

References
1. Weatherford, Jack, The History of Money, Crown Publishers, Inc., 1997.
2. Grabbe, Orlin J., International Financial Markets, 3rd. ed., Prentice Hall.
3. Cohen, Benjamin, Bretton Woods System, http://www.polsci.ucsb.edu/faculty/cohen/inpress/bretton.html
4. Congressional Budget Office, The Budget and Economic Outlook: Fiscal Years 2006 to 2015, released on January 25, 2005.
5. Wiggin, Addison, The Demise of the Dollar, John Wiley & Son, Inc., 2005.
6. U.S. Bureau of Public Debt, The Debt to the Penny and Who Holds It, http://www.publicdebt.treas.gov/opd/opdpdodt.htm
7. U.S. Bureau of Public Debt, Interest Expense on the Debt Outstanding, http://www.publicdebt.treas.gov/opd/opdint.htm
8. CIA World Factbook, http://www.cia.gov/cia/publications/factbook/rankorder/2119rank.html
9. U.S. Census. Bureau, Income, Poverty, and Health Insurance Coverage in the United States, 2004.
10. U.S. Treasury Bulletin, Ownership of Federal Securities, September 2005,
11. http://www.fms.treas.gov/bulletin/index.html
12. Peterson, Peter, G., Running on Empty, Farrar, Straus, and Giroux, 2004.
13. Mühleisen, Martin and Christopher Towe, U.S. Fiscal Policies and Priorities for

14. <u>Long-Run Sustainability</u>, Occasional Paper 227, January 7, 2004 International Monetary Fund.

15. Dowd, Kevin, Too Big to Fail?: Long Term Capital Management and the Federal Reserve, Cato Institute Briefing Papers, Briefing Paper No. 52, September 23, 1999.

16. Congressional Budget Office, CBO's Economic Forecasting Record, October 2005.

17. Congressional Budget Office, CBO's Current Economic Projections, August 15, 2005.

18. Duncan, Richard, <u>The Dollar Crisis, Causes and Consequences</u>, John Wiley & Sons(Asia), 2003.

CHAPTER THREE
The Debt Bomb

It was a cold October day when the seventeen-year-old runaway arrived wet, disheveled, and messy in New Jersey. He had just spent the last of his money on a roll when he was spotted by Deborah Read. There was something about this young fellow that touched young Deborah. When she convinced her father to take in and shelter this fellow, little did she know she would become his wife within several years. The fellow, though young, and one of seventeen siblings, had come from a modest background and had been forced to assume management of a family business and face the challenges of adversity. He had developed skill, initiative. He worked hard and diligently. He'd soon found employment with a local printer as an assistant. It was not long before he gained wider recognition for his aptitudes and received offers of sponsorship for his own business. His skill, hard work, and integrity took him far. Circumstances had separated him from Deborah, and she married another man. Life's twists and turns are strange, however, and after her husband left her and later died an early death, she and this fellow resumed their relationship and became common law husband and wife. In addition to being a good business woman herself, she raised their two children, as well as a child fathered during the years they were apart.

While the description of this family's history would seem not seem to be representative of the story book American family, it signifies the complexity and challenges of many American families, and embodies some of the highest ideals we have held as a free and democratic society. It is well to remember this fellow's famous quote. "A penny earned is a penny saved."

When this fellow, Benjamin Franklin, wrote this as Poor Richard, of <u>Poor Richard's Almanac</u>, he was expressing a value that he had learned from his own real experiences of rising from modest circumstances to a mythical giant of history. The values of hard work, initiative, prudent risk taking through entrepreneurship, and thrift formed the foundation of the United States as it became one of the greatest countries in the world.

While Ben Franklin certainly had talents and skills far beyond those of the ordinary person, his recognition of these fundamental values as a foundation for success had also been discovered by other people who had risen to the challenges of economic adversity. I have been lucky enough to have been able to work with older Americans who had lived through the Great Depression of the 1930's. It etched itself into their lives as an indelible mark. It gave rise to a generation of Americans who bravely embodied the ideals America's founding fathers had in their vision of America. Through the end of the second World War, the courage, hard work, diligence, and thrift of these people had laid the foundation for America's emergence as a twentieth century superpower. However, as the influence of these individuals faded, America forgot to practice the values that had lead to its greatness.

Instead of a nation of savers and investors, we have become a nation of consumers who know no limits. According to a <u>2002 Federal Reserve Bank of San Francisco Letter,</u> the personal savings rate in the United States has fallen sharply. It is at a very low level compared to past savings rates in the U.S. as well as compared to many other industrialized countries. From 1980 until 1994 the U.S. savings rate averaged 8%. From mid 2000 through 2001 it had dropped to 1%. By comparison, from 1980 through 2001 the personal saving rates averaged 13% in Japan, 12% in Germany, and 15% in France.

Not only are Americans not saving enough, they are spending their future earnings. Borrowing to consume today represents a pledge of future earnings for current consumption. Borrowing for consumption purposes may be a useful tool to improve the quality of life when done in an occasional and thoughtful way. When it is a chronic pattern of behavior, it becomes a cumulative financial burden from which it is difficult to emerge, a financially dysfunctional addiction.

People become overly indebted for many reasons. Through my work and experience, I know that economic circumstances sometime leave a growing personal debt burden as one of the only apparent recourses in coping with economic distress. In other cases, a growing personal debt is a result of the failure to restrain one's inclination to indulge in more immediate gratifications. Exercising financially responsible spending decisions on a personal level will certainly be a financial strategy that can improve your financial position and security. I take the position, through my observation of people's spending and consumption decisions, that most people appear unable, or unwilling, to restrain their personal consumption to a level that is financially responsible. When this behavior becomes widespread and acceptable as a normal way of living we have a societal economic behavior that has an impact on the current and future economic and investment landscape. Developing a more clear understanding of what the potential impact of this behavior may be gives us an opportunity to view the investment risks, as well as opportunities, that result from this seemingly established social behavior.

Just how established is this social behavior, and does the evidence support the conclusion of the spendthrift behavior of the American consumer? Apart from my, and possibly your, anecdotal observations of consumer behavior, there is an impressive body of evidence that paints the same picture. The American Bankers Association reported in 2005 that the number of people in the United States who are past due on their credit card payments hit a record in the second quarter of 2005. Delinquency rates also rose for auto loans and home equity loans. According to the U.S. Department of Commerce, Bureau of Economic Analysis, personal savings was a negative 0.2% in October and November of 2005. Negative personal savings means that as a whole Americans are spending more than they are saving. This was in a period of time where economic growth was in the 3.5% range, considered moderately strong. If Americans are having a difficult time making ends meet when the economy is considered relatively strong, the compelling conclusion is that if the economy were to hit a soft patch, or an outright recession, the impact on the average American consumer is likely to be quite severe.

Importantly, a major funding source has allowed this high level of consumption to continue. Interest rates have been low and have permitted easy access to credit. Low interest rates and easy access to credit are a great temporary stimulus to economic growth. Similar to the Japanese economy in the late twentieth century, real estate values have grown rapidly from 2000-2005. Low interest rates and easy access to credit allowed many more participants to qualify to buy property. More participants in the real estate market meant increasing demand. Increasing demand for real estate pushed up property values. Increasing property values meant, on paper at least, real estate owners were becoming wealthier. These owners could then borrow against the increased value of their properties. This borrowing then provided additional money for consumption and investment. The additional consumption enabled by this wealth creation provided the fuel to sustain reasonable economic growth. It has allowed consumers to continue to borrow and purchase consumer goods. Additionally, part of appreciated equity value of real estate had become available as additional investment capital through equity loans. Some of these funds found their way back into the real estate market and had pushed property values up further.

I make reference to the consumer debt, over-consumption, and low savings behavior of the American consumer because of the central place this consumer plays in the American and global economy. He is responsible for approximately two-thirds of the economic growth in the United States. Moreover, since consumption preferences of Americans have swung heavily toward purchasing goods from other countries, much of the developing world economies have depended upon the willingness of Americans to go deeper and deeper into debt to build their economies. Any reasonable person intuitively understands that spending more that what is being earned cannot go on indefinitely. At some point lenders become unwilling to lend. As the debtor's financial situation deteriorates, lenders will demand more interest for what they are lending to compensate themselves for the additional risk of loaning to marginally creditworthy borrowers.

When these circumstances occur on a large social scale, as they currently are, it is important to consider possible outcome scenarios which will impact the investment climate. Three levels of action will shape and impact our financial future—the individual, the U.S. economy, and the global economy.

We will begin at the largest scale, the global level and work down to the individual level. The reason for this approach is my belief that the most powerful and difficult trends to alter are those which are the largest. These are the trends cast the die. This is not to say that it is my belief that the individual is powerless in the face of these mega trends. It is to say that the choices available to the individual exist, and are shaped by, the larger global and domestic economic and political events that are in place. The most effective financial planning and investment strategy must acknowledge and respond to the social and economic conditions likely to be present. The acceptance of the dangerous and static belief that our way of life will remain as we have known it to be will leave multitudes of people poorly prepared to cope with increasingly challenging financial circumstances.

On a global scale the United States has become increasingly dependent on inexpensive and high quality imports to satisfy consumer demand. The flow of U.S. dollars into the countries supplying the U.S. with these goods and services has enabled them to bootstrap themselves into better economic conditions through reinvestment of these dollars into their country. These countries have used surplus dollars, beyond what can be reasonably used without stimulating their economies to overheated conditions, to loan money back to the United States. The dollars that the United States borrows from abroad then becomes available to fund the growing U.S. budget deficit. Because of the availability of these foreign loans to the United States, they have provided the monetary liquidity needed to keep interest rates low.

As we have previously discussed, it is these low interest rates which have allowed, and encouraged, the U.S. consumer to keep borrowing and spending. The low interest rate environment also enabled the recent real estate boom to emerge. When reflecting upon this circumstance, this is a vendor financing situation for the United States. Countries exporting their goods to the United States are the vendors who finance the purchases of the buyer, the United States. The financial well-being of the United States has become dependent upon the willingness of other countries to loan money to the United States. This transfers down to the level of you and me as individuals with our financial well-being determined by the good will, or strategic intentions, of other governments. The right to self-determination, a principle closely associated with being a democratic and free society, is only an exercisable right to the extent it can be paid for. This right has been, and continues to be, steadily sold off by our federal, state, and local governments, as well as ourselves as individuals, by continuing expenditures beyond our means.

How likely is it that foreign countries will stop or decrease their loans to the United States? Through 2004 there have been rumblings thorough media reports of just such an event. South Korea, Russia, and Japan have voiced concern about the vast risk exposure they have because of their accumulations of dollar denominated assets, such as U.S. Treasury debt. The most recent financial tremors have arisen from China in January of 2006. As of the beginning of 2006, China had over $800 billion dollars of foreign currency reserves. Estimates are that by the end of 2006, it will have over $1 trillion dollars of foreign reserves. China's State Administration of Foreign Exchange pledged to "actively explore more efficient use of our foreign exchange reserves." When viewed in the context of Yu Yongdong, an economist with the monetary policy committee of China's central bank, that China's foreign currency reserves are now vulnerable to a drop in the value of the dollar, it sends a strong signal that China has begun to view it in their interests to diversify away from U.S. dollar denominated assets.

Apart from any jockeying for geopolitical position, China has a real economic concern. Recall that the U.S. dollar retains its value by virtue of people's faith in it. It has no inherent value to exchange for goods and services other than this. Demand for U.S. dollars establishes the value of them. If for some reason demand for U.S. dollars were to decrease because people no longer wanted to buy as much goods, services, or investments priced in dollars, the value of the dollar would decrease. If we consider that other countries goods and services are what people of other countries as well as the United States are purchasing, we see a decreasing need for dollars and an increasing need for the currencies of other countries to make these purchases. A saving grace for the U.S. dollar has been that oil has been internationally priced in dollars. Foreign demand for U.S. investments priced in dollars has also held strong, including the purchase of U.S. Treasury debt. Additionally, the central governments of exporting countries, such as Japan, have also intervened in the international currency markets to support a strong dollar against their currencies, as the Yen. This is done, for example, by purchasing dollars with Yen. The result is a stronger dollar relative to the Yen. This is desirable to an exporting country, because it makes the price of its goods less expensive to purchase. A stronger dollar buys more goods priced in a weaker currency relative to the dollar.

Despite the promising U.S. economic news that the government regularly produces, the foundation of the U.S. economic system is crumbling from the current and cumulative budgetary deficits. It is similar to building a magnificent building on a very bad foundation. It may look good and may even stand for awhile. Sooner or later, however, the foundation will give way and the building will crumble. This has not escaped the notice of the more financially savvy policy makers and investors. Despite a stronger dollar during 2005, probably supported by the Federal Reserve interest rate hiking policies, the U.S. dollar has resumed its descent. There have been reports that oil may be priced in Eurodollars instead of, or in addition to, being priced in dollars. Exporting countries, like Japan, who were supporting a strong dollar by their central bank intervention to keep their economies going, are now becoming strong enough so that it is not as necessary to continue purchasing U.S. dollars to strengthen the dollar relative to their own currency. The net result is that the U.S. dollar resumed its decline in 2006. Nevertheless, whether the dollar resumes it slide now or later, it appears that the conditions are present for the U.S. dollar to continue to deteriorate in value.

The implications of a deteriorating dollar value are profound. A decrease in the value of the dollar means that the dollar is able to purchase less and less. Another way of looking at this is that everything becomes more expensive as the dollar becomes worth-less. All of those imported goods and services become more costly as well as oil, energy, raw materials, and food. If you are an exporting country holding a large amount of U.S. dollar denominated investments as a part of your foreign currency reserves, a decline in the value of the U.S. dollar also represents a decline in the value of the investments you are holding that are valued in dollars. As wealth represents an amount of purchasing power, a decline in the value of the dollar represents a decline purchasing power, and consequently a decline in your wealth. If you are concerned about the decline in value of an asset you are holding in your portfolio, it would be most sensible to limit your exposure to the risk of this asset by reducing or otherwise limiting the amount you were holding.

In the case of a country like China, which holds such a huge amount of U.S. dollar denominated investments, there is the problem of creating a self-fulfilling prophecy. The financial impact of China diversifying its foreign currency reserves by reducing its future purchases and/or selling some of its existing holdings could itself set in motion a reduction in the value of the dollar which would make its own portfolio worth less. The problem becomes a problem of the "too big to fail" species. In fact, just the rumor or report of China's intent to reduce its U.S. denominated holdings or reduce their purchase is enough to set in motion downward pressure on the U.S. dollar. This does not mean China will not make a strategic response to this problem, which might take the form of purchasing other assets denominated in U.S. dollars that play a strategic role in China's future well being, yet maintain demand for the dollar for the time being.

What might this look like? China's continuing economic growth depends upon access to sufficient supplies raw materials and energy. If China were to make its U.S. dollars available for the direct purchase and ownership of these assets it will have accomplished at least two strategic objectives. It has secured control over valuable strategic resources, and it has diversified its risk in holding dollar denominated assets such as U.S. Treasury debt. Moreover, China has actually reallocated its wealth to assets which could well benefit from a decline in the value of the U.S. dollar. A decline in the value of the dollar means it takes more dollars to buy raw materials, oil, and other energy resources. That means that ownership of these types of assets become more valuable. When we consider, even without a decline in the value of the U.S. dollar, the growing demand for these resources with respect to a relatively constrained supply, economic circumstances already weigh in favor of an increase in the value of these resource assets.

What can we actually observe about the likelihood of this type strategic response to an over-accumulated U.S. dollar position? In 2005 and 2006 China has already moved to acquire direct ownership of energy and resource interests. Chinese National Offshore Oil Company (CNOOC), the giant Chinese oil company, owned 70% by the Chinese government, tried to buy the American oil company Unocal. Political concern and outrage made this attempt at acquisition of a strategic resource unsuccessful. The world, however, extends beyond the reach of America's borders and control. In early 2006, CNOOC paid $2.3 billion for a 45% stake in a Nigerian oil field. Only days later, media reports stated that CNOOC was preparing to bid for a Kazakhstan oil company. Another way of converting U.S. dollar reserves into other assets is by purchasing gold with dollars and thereby increasing the amount of gold held by the Chinese central bank. The Financial Times reported in January of 2006 of rumors circulating that the Chinese central bank may have already amassed over 1,000 tons of gold reserve holdings, 400 tons more than reported six months earlier.

For an economy, such as that of the United States that is institutionally and individually over-indebted, the prospect of a decrease in the willingness of lenders to continue lending is an ominous sign. The U.S. economy runs on credit, from the federal and state governments down to the level of the individual. Moreover, since much of the developing world's economies have depended upon the U.S. consumer to keep their exporting economies expanding, these economies have been beneficiaries of a relatively strong U.S. economy. The implications of a decrease in available funding for the U.S. economies credit needs would be a slowdown in U.S. economy, and by extension, a likely slowdown in many of the other global economies. A decrease in the willingness to lend money means that the credit markets would drive interest rates higher. Higher interest rates mean that borrowing costs escalate, which means that the debt-serving costs of the U.S government go up. Each time the government has to borrow money, it does so at a greater cost. This increased interest expense becomes part of the federal budget deficit which, in turn, means the federal government needs to borrow even more money at higher interest rates. If the reader is getting the impression that the U.S. government seems to be trapped in a deteriorating economic picture, I believe that to be an accurate impression.

A deteriorating economic picture for the federal government soon translates into the same condition for state and local governments. We need only consider the federal funds that supplement state budgets in the areas of health, education, and welfare, not to mention pork barrel funding that congressional representatives manage to secure for their state constituencies. A deteriorating federal budget has to trickle down to the state and local levels. It is a natural downstream consequence that as the money flow dries up further upstream, there is less available to make it downstream.

A glaring example of the downstream financial distress to state and local governments would be the Medicaid system. Medicaid is a health care system for the poor. The costs of the program are shared by the state and federal governments. The program serves as a social safety net to assure that the neediest citizens have access to some degree of health care. While there are many sound financial reasons this program cannot be financially afforded by state and local governments, this is another of those caught between a "rock and a hard spot" issues. None of the people in the U.S. lives in a social vacuum. How well society cares for its neediest citizens may well be a measure of the quality of our society and our lives. Given how poorly prepared Americans are for what might have been their retirement years, it is likely that a growing number of Americans will be in need of social services, such as health care assistance in the near future. Couple the growing need for these services with a decrease in the available funds to pay for them and we have a picture of an overburdened system. The likely result is the deterioration in the quality of care as well as access to what available care there is. The Federal congress, in 2005 budget deliberations, already started to carve away at Medicaid benefits. This likely means states will have money available from the federal government to cost share on these expenses. Health care, and medical costs, is an entire topic in itself and will be more fully discussed in a chapter of its own. The purpose of introducing it here is merely to illustrate a severe fraying in the social fabric that that many of us have assumed is an entitled part of our way of life. As is the intent of this book, the personal and financial implications of this larger global issue are of particular interest. What are the implications of this overwhelming burden of debt at the governmental and personal levels, and what does it mean to us as individuals? What are the preparations we should be making to defend ourselves from the potential implications of this situation? More specifically, where might be the risks and opportunities unfold?

If we are watching a potentially severe economic crisis in the United States, we need to look at other countries that have experienced severe economic crises in order to get a better understanding of what we might expect. Until the late 1990's Argentina had one of the strongest economies in Latin America, as measured by Gross Domestic Product (GDP). They had a large middle class and relatively affluent sector. Culturally rich and diverse, Buenos Aires, the capital, was know as the "Paris" of the southern hemisphere. The Teatro Colon, completed at the beginning of the twentieth century, rivaled the best opera houses in Europe. The Museum of Fine Arts housed the works of the world's master artists, such as Picasso, Rembrandt, and Renoir. Italian marble statues and fresco's lined the walls of subway stations throughout the city. The Peronist political movement had made access to health care and education available to everyone. Looking at this picture, appearances would suggest Argentina to be a democratic, prosperous, and modern country. The problem, however, was that this picture was built upon a mountain of debt. By the late 1990's, the debt had become so overwhelming that it brought about a severe economic crisis. From 1998-2002 Argentina's economy shrank by 25% with a sharp devaluation in their currency. The country was thrown into an extreme political, social, and economic upheaval resulting in the evaporation of financial position and security for most households. To make matters even worse for these Argentine families, for a period of time the Argentine government put restrictions on gaining access to whatever wealth these families had left after the currency devaluation.

While there are certainly differences between Argentina and the United States, the road to financial hell can be reached by many different routes. Once there, however, basic economics, and the universality of some human behaviors, suggest that the experiences of these Argentine families would illuminate our future in the U.S. A study produced by the World Bank Office for Argentina, Chile, Paraguay, and Uruguay looked at the impact of the Argentine crisis on household welfare with the deterioration in social conditions, increases in poverty, deterioration in the health and education sector with regard to delivery of services, and increases and levels of crime and violence.

By May of 2002, Argentina's unemployment rate had reached over 21%. The loss was particularly severe in the area of unskilled jobs and construction jobs. Many of the other jobs that remained were jobs of reduced quality with loss of benefits. The poverty rate had increased to over 50% of the Argentine population. The combinations of factors from these upheavals lead to increasingly conflictive social situations. These in turn, lead to increased crime and violence. As I recall from reading in the media reports during these events, it appeared that kidnapping became a cottage industry. The overall subjective welfare, which is how people felt about the future, was of increasing discouragement and pessimism. The overwhelming reasons for these feelings were economic.

The strategies Argentine households used to personally respond to their country's socio-economic crisis were characterized the by World Bank study as being adaptive, active, or social networking. They are basic enough strategies so that we might expect they would also be used were the United States to descend into a severe economic crisis. The adaptive strategy would be changing consumption patterns by consuming less and/or substituting less expensive goods than what was preferred. This might mean reduced food consumption, substituting less expensive foods, not being able to buy needed medicines, and switching to less expensive methods of transportation such as public transportation, or walking or bicycling. The active strategy would involve such things as selling assets, using savings, borrowing, or relocating to where opportunities are perceived to be better. It might also involve home production of food for consumption and/or sale to others. Pawning or mortgaging personal belongings, as well as trying to work more hours, would also be a part of this strategy. The social network strategy would be to receive support from family or friends, receive public support from whatever government programs might be available, using bartering as a means of exchange of value, or participating in communal activities such as school meal programs, and neighborhood or community meal programs.

These strategies are all reactive strategies in response to trying to survive and make the best of an undesirable set of circumstances. Most of us in the United States would not voluntarily elect to employ these strategies if we had other alternatives. I suspect the same was true for the Argentines who were forced, by circumstances beyond their individual control, to do what was necessary to take care of themselves and their families. The best way to avoid being pressured into having to elect undesirable choices is to adopt a proactive strategy that allows you to be better prepared should circumstances beyond your control prevail in creating financial hardship The dictum plan for "plan for the worse, and hope for the best" is as relevant as ever today, if not more so.

My subjective opinion of the aftermath of the Argentine financial crisis was formed during my stay in Buenos Aires during the summer of 2005. Argentina had begun the rebuilding process and their economy was improving. I found riding the subway in Buenos Aires, called the Sub T, gave me a very good look at a large cross section of the residents. As I looked at the expressions and demeanor on the middle aged and older people, I saw a subdued resignation in their circumstances. It appeared as if they were awakening from an economic shell shock and were realizing that much of what they had anticipated as being a secure financial future had evaporated. Their savings and pensions were lost or seriously diminished. Their outlook was the belief that they were too old to rebuild their financial lives and make whole the dreams that hand been shattered by the Argentine financial crisis. On the other hand, the younger people seemed to be lively and enthusiastic about their future prospects. They knew that they had their lives ahead of them. Middle aged or older persons need more time to collect themselves and reconstruct their lives after a serious setback, financial or otherwise. Ideally, it would be best to adopt a proactive strategy to minimize the damage from the potentially disastrous financial events which appears to be likely in the future of the United States.

The foundation of a proactive financial strategy is accumulating savings and investments. The benefit of electing this strategy is that even if the United States does not descend into a full blown financial crisis, despite the evidence that it appears on track to do so, accumulating savings and investments is something that will make your future financial quality of life more secure in any case. Unfortunately, however, the overall behavior of people in the United States suggests a very low regard for saving. Saving and investing implies a willingness to defer some degree of gratification to a future date. We have become a culture of immediate, or as close to immediate gratification, as possible. The overwhelming messages bombarding us, from every direction, from the sides of our paper coffee cups to full-scale programming infomercials, is to consume. From the way our system is constructed, the economic well-being of our society and that of the individual appear to be in direct conflict with one another. Consumption is what drives economic growth in our society. Consumption is what fuels the need for employees to produce goods and services to supply the demands of the consumer. The more the consumer spends, however, the poorer they become. As savings and investments decline and consumption continues, not only are today's dollars spent, tomorrow's dollars are spent as well. This means that if and when a financial crisis occurs on a larger economic scale or because of personal circumstances, the less prepared one is to cope with these adverse circumstances, and the more desperate the situation becomes. Choices and alternatives diminish as financial resources decrease.

On the other hand, if people save and invest more and consume less, economic growth slows. Slowing economic growth means higher unemployment and greater social financial distress, both on the larger social scale and at the level of the individual. We appear to have a type of schizophrenic social economic system that leads to "damned if you do, and damned if you don't" as far and spending and consumption decisions go. Obviously, this is a dysfunctional situation that cannot continue indefinitely. The ultimate financial breakdowns of this system will cause global economic disruption. Fortunately, however, individual choice still provides an opportunity to create shelter from the coming storm. While the vast majority of people will likely be unable or unwilling to modify their behaviors to better prepare them for tomorrow, there will be those people who do decide to better prepare themselves. Not only will these people be better prepared to weather the harsher financial climate we will likely encounter, they will also be more able to capitalize on the opportunities that arise in adverse economic climates, for those who have the resources to do so. Fire sale pricing in the need to sell assets during times of financial distress leads to the opportunity to acquire good, solid, undervalued assets at very favorable prices. While we may be looking at monumental financial crisis in the future of the United States, the other side of then coin is that we may also be looking at a monumental investment opportunity as well, if we are prepared for it.

The question, then, is what is we must do to prepare, both for the potential downside as well as the potential opportunities on the upside. Being economically overburdened and having to service debt is a financial killer. It weakens your ability to survive adverse circumstances by draining away your financial lifeblood. Before you can thrive, you have to survive. If you have kept your debt burden low, or non-existent, good for you. While there is an appropriate use of, and amount of, debt from a financial management point of view, it has become such a cultural addiction. One should exercise extreme caution in assuming debt. It is comparable to alcoholism where there is no such thing as just one drink. The first task in strengthening yourself financially is to stop the financial hemorrhage. The appropriate strategy when you find yourself in a hole, it not to stay the course. It is to stop digging.

The implications are comparable to going through the type of withdrawal experienced by other addictions. It will not be pleasant. It may mean depriving yourself of indulgences to which you have become accustomed as a routine part of your life. You may find yourself irritable and angry. While unpleasant, however, you should keep in mind that to electively make a decisive choice to change behaviors that are damaging to your well being, you are affirming the power you have in your own life to have some control over your future. The alternative is to continue dysfunctional financial behavior that will likely also result in your being deprived of the indulgences which you consider to be a routine part of your life. In that case, however, it will likely be imposed upon you. Saying no to purchasing decisions that are robbing you of your future is your first step in establishing a stronger foundation for your future.

The next step, if you find yourself in a financial hole, is to dig yourself out of it. This will also not be pleasant. Depending upon how deeply you are in debt, bankruptcy or restructuring your debt to be more manageable given your resources may be one consideration. Other alternatives could be selling nonproductive assets and applying the proceeds to debt reduction, working more with an additional job, or more hours, or reducing other regular expenditures. It is your life and you make your own decisions. The best advice is of no use if the willingness to implement it is not exercised. It is neither the intention nor the mission of the writer to attempt to coddle the reader into believing there some magic strategy that will make the difficulty and unpleasantness of being overly indebted disappear.

Once the financial hemorrhaging, and blood loss, is under control, the process of building can begin. If you have not done a very good job saving and investing, you must adopt the perspective of having this become a central theme in your life. Many people seem to have adopted an inherently self-contradictory attitude about money where its importance is diminished with regard to saving, but not with regard to spending. The spending impulse needs to be refocused with the same intensity directed towards saving and investing for your future. Find the same joy in each dollar you can save for your future as in that latte, wine, or dessert, by remembering that for each of those dollars you are setting aside for your future, you are claiming your right to be more in charge of your life.

At this point, wise saving and investment choices are imperative. Many marketers and marketing organizations would have you believe that you merely have to go to their website and within minutes you will have many different investment ideas. Alternatively, a popular notion is that you can go to top rated packaged investments like mutual funds, plunk you money down, and not do too much thinking beyond that. Then again, you can sign up for one of the investment programs with inane witticisms, such as to only buy stocks when they are going up, or teaching you how you can, with the help of their high tech software programs, be a master stock technician knowing when the right times are to buy and sell. While some of these systems may have some grain of truth, if investing were that easy, everyone with half a brain would be well off. In my experience as a professional advisor and investor with over fifteen years of practice, experience, and thousands of hours of continuing education, nothing seems to work all the time. Some things work some times and not others. The only way I have seen that seems to help make better investment decisions is paying attention and thinking critically about events in the world and their implications for you.

On that basis, the mega-trend of governmental and personal over-indebtedness is huge and defines a high probability of large scale financial disruption. Financial institutions such as insurance companies, banks, and related businesses are likely to feel the brunt. An economic slowdown as a result of an inability to continue consuming at the previous levels that have sustained economic growth would be felt by retailers and manufacturers of goods that are purchased with discretionary income or debt. These types of companies are to be avoided if one were looking at constructing a defensive portfolio. Companies and investments which are producers of non-discretionary goods and services would have more resistance to an economic downturn. Food, agriculture, energy, raw materials, and commodities would be good examples and the types of economic sectors that may continue to prosper as a result of continuing demand from Asia, China and India in particular. Additionally, a deterioration of the current monetary system of the United States and other countries operating with fiat currencies will likely result in demand for gold and silver to resume their historical role as stores of economic value. We would expect to see strong demand and higher prices in this area for some time to come.

References

1. A Quick Biography of Ben Franklin, The Electric Ben Franklin, www.U.S.history.org/franklin/info/index.htm.

2. What's Behind the Low Savings Rate, FRBSF Economic Letter, Number 2002-09, March 29, 2002.

3. Kelley, Rob, CNN/Money staff writer, Debt: consumers juggle big burden, CNN.com, October 10, 2005.

4. Lagomarsino, Deborah, Credit Card Delinquencies Hit High in Second Quarter, Dow Jones Newswires, September 28, 2005, 10:45 a.m.

5. Calmes, Jackie, New Programs Spur Working Poor To Begin Saving, Wall Street Journal, January 11, 2006.

6. Personal Income and Outlays: November 2005, Bureau of Economic Analysis, U.S. Department of Commerce, December 22, 2005.

7. Goodman, Peter, China Set to Reduce Exposure to Dollar, Washington Post, January 10, 2005.

8. Flood, Chris, Oil Edges Higher on Iran and Nigeria Concerns, Financial Times, January 16, 2006.

9. Consuming concern: why the stamina of shoppers will be crucial for global growth, Comment and Analysis, Financial Times, January 20, 2006.

10. Fizbein, Ariel, et. al., Argentina's crisis and its impact on household welfare, The World Bank Office for Argentina, Chile, Paraguay, and Uruguay, Working Paper N.1/02, November 2002.

CHAPTER FOUR
The Pension Fiasco

I recently worked with a couple considering retirement. The fellow had worked for the same company for thirty years. As part of the benefits program from his employer, a pension was offered to reward and retain employees for years of dedication and loyalty to the company. Having recently turned fifty-five, this fellow was eligible for an early retirement. Though not wealthy, by most standards the couple had done well. They had no debt except for a small remaining mortgage on their residence. They had an investment property which they intended to sell after retirement as well as some additional retirement investments. The major source of funding for retirement income was to come from the employer's pension plan and, at age sixty-seven, Social Security. Based upon what this couple believed their estimated retirement income needs would be, it appeared to them that they would be able to anticipate a financially secure retirement. They came to me to validate and confirm their views on this. After analyzing their circumstances, I was left with a number of serious reservations regarding their retirement plans. While not the only problem, the most significant source of concern to me was the lifetime income promised from the company's pension plan.

It is important to become familiar with the types of pension plans in order to understand where this couple, and millions more like them, are directly at risk. Two broad categories of pension plans are government pension plans and company pension plans. Examples of government pensions plans would be Social Security, or the various state pension plans. While them, with promised benefits to millions of people, often cause for concern, our attention at this juncture will be directed towards the company pension plans. Two broad types of company pension plans are what are known as defined contribution pension plans and defined benefit pensions. A familiar type of defined contribution plan is known as a 401(k). This plan is called a defined contribution plan because the only the amount of allowable contribution is specified by the plan. The actual retirement benefit will depend upon whether or not the allowable contributions are made and what the resulting investment performance would be.

Defined benefit pension plans are a different breed. While offered by fewer and fewer companies, they had been the traditional pension plans. They still provide retirement benefits for millions current retirees with promised benefits to millions more future retirees. They are called defined benefit plans because they spell out what retirement income benefit the employee will receive at retirement after fulfilling their employee roles. A defining benefit formula might be some percentage of the last five years average earned income. The percentage might be based upon the number of years of employment with the company. For example, let's say a company's defined benefit plan offers a 2% retirement income benefit accumulation for each year an employee is with the company. The accumulated percentage is applied to the last five years of average compensation of the employee to determine the amount of retirement income benefit. If an employee worked with the company for thirty years and had a final five year average salary of $70,000, they could expect a retirement income of 60% of $70,000, or $42,000 per year. The benefit is usually offered as some type of annuity, or monthly income stream. Often this is a fixed income, which in an inflationary environment is a problem if the recipient plans on living for a while. Significant as this problem is, it is not the focus of our attention at this time.

The primary strength of this traditional type pension plan is the promise of a baseline income to a retired worker, as adequate or inadequate as that may be. Promises can be broken, and unfortunately, often are. With over 44 million employees participating in these plans, it would become a serious public policy issue if the financial foundation of these plans were to become weakened by poor management or malfeasance. As a well intentioned response to this concern, Congress passed the Employee Retirement Income Security Act in 1974, known as ERISA. This act was intended to provide protection and regulation to the promises made to employees participating in these plans. One of the concerns of this act was to protect an employee's retirement if a company sponsoring one of these plans was to go bankrupt. As a result the Pension Benefit Guaranty Corporation, known as PBGC, was created to insure these plans in case a company sponsoring these plans became insolvent.

As of year 2005, the PBGC has had to assume responsibility for almost 3,600 pension plans that ended, which represents payment of retirement income to over 683,000 retirees. At present, PBGC owes retirement income benefits to the current and future pensions of 1.3 million people. This figure will rise as more pension plans end. When a pension plan ends, a maximum income benefit will be paid to the plan's retirees. This amount is adjusted each year. For plans that ended in 2005, the maximum benefit that would be paid to a plan retiree was a little over $3,800 a month.

Naturally, if the PBGC is insuring pension plans and paying out income benefits to retirees, it must have a source of funding with which to pay these benefits. The PBGC receives no funding from general tax revenues, and its promises are not backed by the United States Government. The way in which it raises money to pay benefits is by changing an insurance premium to companies insuring their pension through the PBGC. The amount of premium the PBGC may charge is set by Congress. Although this seems a sensible way to run this type of program, serious problems have arisen in its implementation.

As of the middle of November 2005, the PBGC had a deficit of over 23 billion dollars. This means it had obligation to pay income benefits that were 23 billion dollars more than its means. During 2005, PBGC took over the pensions of 120 company plans that were in trouble. Because of the way government regulations allow pension liabilities to be accounted for, companies are able to game the system to under fund their pension plans. If those companies later get into financial trouble and the PBGC has to take over their plan, the PBGC is responsible covering the under funding of the plan up to the maximum benefit payout specified by law. Of the 102 pension plans taken over by PBGC in 2005, the average plan was only 50% funded. By the PBGC's own estimate, there is a high probability of new additional plan terminations. PBGC believes its additional exposure amount for new likely plan terminations to be approximately 108 billion dollars.

The Congressional Budget Office, known as the CBO, is a small non-partisan agency of the Federal Government. Their mandate is to provide objective and impartial assistance to the House and Senate Budget Committees in the budgetary process by preparing reports and analyses on issues likely to affect Federal budgetary decisions. In recent years the transfer of several large airline and steel company pension plans to the PBGC has raised concern about the possible impact of events such as these on the federal budget. Under current law the PBGC is supposed to be self funded from its operations. There was obviously growing alarm that if it were necessary for the PBGC to take over additional large under-funded pension plans, their own solvency would be called into question. If this were to occur, the impact on the lives of the people participating in these plans would be so great that it would become a public policy issue and, consequently, a political issue requiring Federal intervention. Federal intervention often means dollars directly out of the Federal budget.

When an issue means dollars coming out of the Federal budget, the issue no longer impacts only the people directly participating in these pension plans but every American, because these dollars need to come from somewhere. If they are borrowed, an already huge federal debt becomes worse causing upward pressure on interest rates and a dampening effect on economic growth. If economic growth slows, it means less tax revenues taken in by the federal government, which would result in a reduction in government expenditures and/or an increase in taxes to raise revenues. However, with the limitation of how much taxes can be increased to raise revenues even if there were the political will, the likelihood of meaningful federal expenditure reduction appears remote given the historically demonstrated behavior of the public and their politically representatives.

Unfortunately, in September of 2005, the CBO completed a study called the Risk Exposure of the Pension Benefit Guaranty Corporation. They found that it is likely that the PBGC has under-estimated the amount by which they are under funded as an insurer of these traditional pension plans. At the time of the study, the PBGC estimate of their obligations to retirees from plans taken over by them was $23.3 billion. The CBO estimates that a more realistic accumulated deficit over the next 10 years is closer to $86.7 billion. Over the next 15-20 years the CBO estimate is an accumulated deficit of $119-$141.9 billion.

The trend does not look promising. Companies sponsoring these traditional types of pension plans have an estimated total under funding of $450 billion. While the PBGC expects many of these companies to make good on their pension commitments, at the end of fiscal year 2000 the PBGC reported a surplus of $9.7 billion. By September of 2004 the PBGC had reported a deficit of $23.3 billion. If economic and business conditions were to deteriorate, more of these companies with under-funded pension plans would possibly try to turn them over to the PBGC. According to PBGC Executive Director Bradley Belt, "Unfortunately, the financial health of the PBGC is not improving, the money available to pay benefits is eventually going to run out unless Congress enacts comprehensive pension reform to get plans better funded and provide and provide the insurance program with additional resources." Legislation to reform the pension system being considered by Congress aims to require companies with these types of pension plans to have their plans more fully funded. In addition, the considered legislation would increase premiums paid to the PBGC for insuring their pension plans. The problem with these remedies is that they may make the situation worse. Many companies with large under-funded pension plans are on shaky financial ground themselves. Forcing these companies to redirect their cash flows into more fully funding their pension plans may cause their ongoing business operations to deteriorate further, which would likely accelerate their being taken over by the PBGC as these companies head for bankruptcy. Moreover, increasing the premiums companies pay to the PBGC for insuring their pensions would result in more companies terminating this type of pension plan. Once these plans were terminated, the companies would no longer need to pay premiums to the PBGC, leaving fewer paying companies. The problem goes deeply into the structure of the system that will not be solved by simple solutions.

General Motors is a good example of the difficulties facing the companies sponsoring these traditional types of pension plans. General Motors was once a pillar of American industrial and financial strength that could be depended upon as a prudent investment. In October of 2005, its credit worthiness was again lowered by the independent credit rating agency Standard and Poor's with growing speculation that General Motors may have to file for bankruptcy within several years. What happened to this giant of American industry has occurred in many other institutions and is representative of the American economic system. During the twentieth century, America and its businesses emerged as the economic leaders of the world. As their power and affluence grew, American and its workers naturally wanted a larger slice of the growing economic pie. The result was that through labor contract negotiations companies made pension promises to workers which are now coming due. Because of loopholes in how companies could account for funding their pension promises, they did not in actuality put money away to pay for these promises. In effect, two sets of records to account for pension promises exist; one is the officially sanctioned fictitious version, and the other is the economic reality. Fictions are like mirages; they tend to vanish as the facts of reality assert themselves. That is what happened at General Motors.

Although General Motors claims it pensions to be fully funded, outsiders believe that the firm's pension obligations to be under funded by $31 billion. Under funding of other pension costs, such as retiree health care, are estimated by industry analysts to be as high as $70 billion. General Motors may also be liable for up to an additional $11 billion of pension fund obligations from the recent bankruptcy filing of Delphi, its auto parts supplier. In 1999, when General Motors spun off Delphi as a separate company, GM made some guarantees to assist in case Delphi ever came under financial distress. Based on its 2005 stock market valuations, General Motors is worth $15 billion. These are what are referred to as legacy costs that the company must carry along and factor in as an ongoing cost of doing business. This means that each car GM produces has an additional cost of $1,500 built in to cover these legacy costs. The automobile market is very competitive regarding price and value. In recent years GM has had to offer discounted pricing in order to sell cars, which does not help GM's overall business position. Such a practice may increase sales, but the profit that the company makes decreases. What GM really needs is to increase its profitability. However, it does not seem to be able to come up with a business strategy that inspires much confidence. Moreover, even with its discounted pricing, General Motors is still experiencing sluggish sales, at best.

General Motors is part of a larger problem of the pension system. Ford Motor company has similar problems, as do the airlines and steel companies. The frequency of high profile bankruptcies has caused some of the stigma to fade. From a business perspective, filing bankruptcy and reorganizing a company can leave it a leaner and more competitive business, as is the case with the steel industry bankruptcy filings. The relief from the legacy costs of pension and health care commitments to pensioners by filing bankruptcy has economic implications that go beyond the specific businesses, which is especially true when the filing of bankruptcy becomes a routine strategic business decision. In the case of pensions insured by the PBGC, the pension obligations of these companies become the obligations of the PBGC. Ultimately, unless the U.S. government is willing to allow the PBGC to default, these unfunded pensions are likely to become an additional obligation to the already overburdened U.S. budget and consequently the citizens of the U.S.

References referring to a prospective pension insolvency crisis as the next "Savings and Loan" type bailout by the Federal government are becoming more prevalent. As a refresher on the Savings and Loan Crisis, in 1986 the Federal Savings and Loan Insurance Corporation (FSLIC) became insolvent. Because of corporate malfeasance and mismanagement, the number of Savings and Loan failures was too great for the insurer to adequately cover. Similar to the Pension Benefit Guaranty Corporation, the Federal Savings and Loan Insurance Corporation was supposed to be self-funded with no taxpayer costs. The impact, however, of millions of S&L depositors being financially ruined because of a failure of the Savings and Loan insurer would have been too great a shock to the American financial system. Consequently, Congress stepped in to bail out the FSLIC with the assistance of the U.S. taxpayer. By 1995 the bailout had cost over $150 billion. Explicit in the approach of the government was a belief in the too big to fail. However, fewer and fewer businesses and institutions are too big to fail, because many more large companies and institutions are becoming more marginal in their financial conditions. The financial reality is that even the United States does not have unlimited financial resources. We do, however, seem to have an unlimited ability to use them.

Given this snapshot of these defined benefit, or traditional, type pension plans, let's return to our couple considering early retirement. They were considering basing their financial future on the promise of their employer's defined benefit pension plan, a traditional type pension plan, to pay a guaranteed retirement income. This income would have represented a significant part of their expected retirement income. There are a number of the potential weaknesses with this plan. These weaknesses highlight some of the risks that could compromise the retirement years of this couple.

Let's start with the implicit expected guarantee of receiving this retirement income. These clients were in their mid-fifties. If they took an early retirement, it would likely mean thirty to thirty-five years of retirement income needed. Even assuming their employer was in good financial condition today, and assuming their pension plan was well funded, thirty to thirty-five years is a very long time in today's business environment, which is becoming more competitive. In recent years we have witnessed the deterioration of what were once institutions of American business. It reasonable to expect that as China, India, and other global lower-operating cost businesses become more able to provide products and services to the rest of the world, nothing is off the table with respect to the continued viability of existing and established business. Recent corporate actions, as exemplified by the steel, airline, and automotive industries, show that these existing and established businesses with high legacy costs, such as pension and health care promises, are among the least competitive. They are among the most likely to under fund, terminate, or become insolvent. While bankruptcy reorganization may leave these companies more competitive if they can get out from under their pension and healthcare promises, it leaves their retirees in an uncertain financial position. A prudent individual retirement strategy would take this possibility into consideration.

Several strategic retirement planning responses are possible for our early retirement couple to consider. A reasonably healthy person can anticipate thirty-five to forty years of retirement begun at age fifty-five. However, two significant financial hazards need to be considered with this early retirement strategy. The first hazard is a natural consideration from our discussion above about the weakening financial picture for defined benefit pensions in general. The attractive feature about this type of pension plan is its "guarantee" of a lifetime income. Guarantees are only as good as the guarantor. Fifteen or twenty years ago, very few people would have seriously considered that General Motors would not able to make good on its pension promises. At the present time, discussions concerning the possibility of General Motors filing for bankruptcy within several years with its bonds downgraded to junk bond status have occurred. Should General Motors not be able to meet its pensions promises to its retirees, the Pension Benefit Guarantee Corporation (PBGC) may be able to step in and provide some sort of a safety net for GM's retirees. On the other hand, given the increasingly insolvent condition of the PBGC because of many other companies in General Motors condition, maybe the PBGC won't be available to help. A prudent planning consideration for someone retiring with a defined benefit pension, or traditional type of pension plan, cannot assume with complete peace of mind that this source of retirement is reliable.

A natural response to this condition of retirement income uncertainty would be to try to develop an alternative potential source of retirement income should the pension plan promises become unreliable. In the case of the couple in this example, they could defer retirement for several more years and make it a top priority to save and accumulate additional retirement funds as a financial cushion should their promised pension start to appear shaky. They could develop a business or work part-time during retirement. Depending upon their overall financial circumstances and preferences they may find many other strategies as well.

Another consideration of this couple's early retirement predicament, and one that will likely be faced by anyone participating in these types of defined benefit retirement plans, is that even if the company makes good on its pension promises, the income benefit is usually offered as a monthly fixed income over the lifetime of the retiree and or spouse. This annuity type of income, while possibly offering peace of mind in the appearance of a reliable monthly income, may be nothing more than a sure way of gradually deteriorating the financial standard of living. If there is no cost of living adjustment built in to the promised monthly income, every year the monthly income will be able to purchase less and less. Over a period of fifteen to twenty years, this reduction in purchasing power can become quite significant. For example, even with a moderately low rate of inflation of 3.5% per year, $2,500 of monthly income would have to be adjusted upwards to just under $4,200 per month in fifteen years to buy the same standard of living it can purchase today.

We can see that there are two major problems with these defined benefit pension plans. The first problem is whether or not the guarantor of the promised income will really be able to deliver on its promise. By looking at the company and institutional problems associated with these types of retirement plans, it is becoming more and more of a serious concern that these promises may not be able to be delivered. The other major problem with these defined benefit type pension plans is that even if the income promises are able to be honored, the fixed income nature of these promises may mean a steady deterioration of the financial standard of living for those retirees depending upon the income from these plans. For those retirees without adequate supplemental financial resources, this will likely mean becoming more dependent upon the government at a time when the government cannot afford additional social program expenditures.

These corporate defined benefit pensions are only one of the significant components of the pension problem facing America. Aside from these corporate-defined benefit pension plans, millions of more Americans will be depending upon state and municipality pension promises for their retirement incomes. Unfortunately, the funding situation with these plans is also quite disturbing. They are under-funded by hundreds of millions of dollars. Unlike the corporate defined benefit plans, these governmental pension plans are not insured by an agency like the Pension Benefit Guarantee Corporation. E.J. McMahon, a budget expert at the conservative research group, the Manhattan Institute, summarizes the state and municipality pension problem saying, "If nothing is done to bring pensions under control, all the other headaches that state governments will be facing in the next 20 years on needs like education and health will be enormously worse." Some glaring examples of the magnitude of the problem can be seen in the more than $30 billion shortfall of the New Jersey pension program, as estimated by Otto Kramer, chairman of the $70 billion pension fund. One of the problems that give rise to this type of pension fund shenanigan is the inadequacy of the rules for pension fund accounting. As Kramer says, "Actuarial science [on which pensions are based] involves accounting constructs which are economic fictions and don't mesh with reality. First, when they determine what the assets of the fund are, they look at the average over the past five years. As an investment manager, no investor has ever called me to ask their average account balance over the last five years. People want to know what their account is worth today. Second, the actuaries assume that as people retire they are not replaced in the work force. And third, they used overly optimistic estimates for future returns."

As if this rigged accounting system isn't enough of a headwind for state and municipal pension fund solvency, allegations of mismanagement and corruption plague the pension funding mechanism. In February of 2005, the San Diego City Attorney found that the mayor and several former and current council members violated securities law by endorsing disclosures about the city's finances they knew to be false. These false financial disclosures stemmed from trying to avoid, what the City Attorney Mike Aguirre estimated to be, a $150 million lump sum payment into the pension program because of its severe under-funding.

The general opinion among informed policy makers and their advisors is that the main problem with these state pension programs is that their benefits are too generous. Remedies put on the table to address these problems often take the form of benefit reductions or delaying of retirement age. Needless to say the recipients of these promised pension benefits don't feel the same way. They feel they are entitled to what they have been promised. Indeed, many of these promised pension benefits have their roots in past labor contract negotiations where there was some sort of trade-off between wages and a future pension promise. As with many social and economic problems in our complex world, this appears to be one of those intractable problems. It may be that both responsible policy makers and pension benefit recipients are both right in their viewpoints. Will these pension benefit recipients willingly give up what they believe they are rightly entitled to?

State and other civil service workers represent a very large and organized voting and economic block. The recent transit workers strike in New York City is a good representation of the response to any attempt to try to cut or reduce state pension benefits. This strike, which shut down the largest mass transit system in the country, arose after the Metropolitan Transit Authority tried to increase the retirement age of its workers, or have the workers contribute more into their pension plan. An increase in the amount a worker needed to contribute into their pension plan would have to come from present day wages, which would have meant a reduction in the present day standard of living. On the other hand, The Metropolitan Transit Authority, a state agency, was alarmed that the pension costs for its workers had tripled from 2002 to 2005 to $453 million. The strike has ended. Labor has been successful in having the demand by the Transit Authority management to reduce benefits withdrawn.

I do not begrudge whatever hard-fought-for gains any party may win. As a reminder, this book is not intended to be a prescription for public policy reform or any other type of attempt at saving the world. The objective of this book is much more mundane. It is simply to identify the likely hazards in the economic environment which may directly impact your current and future financial circumstances, and develop a proactive strategy regarding these potentially adverse events. While this may be hailed as a victory by the Transit Workers, it may be more of a Pyrrhic victory. What appears to have been won in pension benefits can be taken away by others means. Higher taxation, or inflation, are two examples of how these benefits can be really be lost despite their appearance of having been won.

It may be politically unfeasible to resolve this pension funding dilemma through the public policy change of benefit reduction. The most likely available recourse to state governments and municipalities to fund these pension promises will be to increase revenues through higher taxation. States do not have the ability to create more money the way the Federal government can. Many states are required by law to have a balanced budget. When state expenses exceed state revenues, state legislatures must cut expenses and/or increase revenues. Expenses can only be cut down to essential services and mandatory expenses, such as payment of pension benefits. At this point a state faces little other choice than increasing its revenues. The primary sources of state revenue are from income, property, and sales taxation. The impact on our individual lives is likely to be deterioration in the amount and quality of services and social infrastructure provided by state governments. State residents may have to be prepared to pick up a greater share of responsibility, and financial expenditure, for services previously provided by the state. The areas where states have traditionally exercised their domain are health, safety, and education. We might reasonably expect that these would be the areas state residents would need to supplement financially if they want to retain their standards of living in these areas. At the same time as these services are deteriorating, state residents may also be compelled to pay more through increased taxation. Inevitably, state residents will be paying more for less.

If this scenario does develop, it is likely to come at a time when the American consumer and retiree are already over-indebted. Additionally, one of the areas of wiggle room for pension benefits appears to be health care benefits. More and more cost shifting to the recipient of these benefits is occurring. The likely outcome of this configuration of economic circumstances suggests that the impact to your financial circumstances will be higher taxes, increasing health care costs, and a reduction of the purchasing power of your income because of escalating inflationary pressures. When we remember the context of this potentially reduced standard of living, it becomes all the more alarming. Recall that those demographic stages of life we are looking at are the senior years of life. This is a stage of life in which our physical and mental capacities will decline. We will become less and less able to depend upon these resources as assets to assist us in our lives. We will become more and more dependent upon the financial resources we have managed to accumulate to work for ourselves during our retirement years. In the absence of adequate financial resources, we will become more and more dependent upon the resources of the government and the goodwill of others who may be able to assist us. As we have seen in our discussion about the already huge Federal budget deficit and accumulating Federal debts, the resources of the government are already stretched beyond what is financially feasible. The resources of whatever social safety net we may now believe to be in place will become increasingly more frayed as millions of Americans entering their retirement years find themselves to be financially poorly prepared. Decreased access to social services and diminished quality of services will be offered. Our government cannot now afford its already promised social benefits, and it will be less likely to afford them in the future. You are likely to be on your own, at a time when your physical, mental, and financial resources are diminishing and stretched.

We have looked at an impending pension debacle with regard to corporate and public service defined benefit type pension plans. The remaining area of pension income for today and tomorrow's retiree is the 401(k) type plan, more generically know as a defined contribution pension plan, which has been replacing the more traditional type of defined benefit pension plan we have been discussing. These are a more attractive pension offering for businesses, because the risk of funding is shifted to the worker. As the generic description of this pension plan suggests, only the amount of allowable contribution in this type of plan is specified. The amount of actual pension benefit depends on how much the employer and/or the employer contribute and how well the investments in this 401(k) type plan perform. These are generally self-directed plans with the employees making the investment selections. To the extent employees do participate in these plans, they are most often poorly prepared to be their own investment advisors. These plans are usually provided by self-interested vendors who provide perfunctory investor education literature, or whose sales representatives who have met the minimal requirements to become a broker's sales representative. They have little real substance to offer other than to parrot prescribed corporate sales scripts. The employee is often left with a simplistic impression of how easy it is to make sound investment decisions with platitudes like "stocks always go up in the long run". The net effect is that for those employees who do choose to participate in these plans, they receive very little real guidance in their investment decision making.

The reality of these pension plans is that, while they have the potential to be a useful and substantial component of a retiree's financial foundation, they are generally misused or under-used. The amount of assets accumulated by these plans is far below what it needs to be.

While it may seem comforting to believe that this is someone else's problem if you do not participate in one of these pension programs, or if you are participating and doing reasonably well, the reality is that we do not live in an economic vacuum. The poor financial decisions of others, especially on a large scale, will impact everyone in the economic system. It is similar to driving. We may be safe and conscientious drivers and reduce our likelihood of becoming involved in an accident. Unfortunately, not all drivers are safe and conscientious. They may involve us in their irresponsible behavior despite our best efforts to avoid them. We must acknowledge this possibility, and if we are prudent, insure against this possibility to minimize our loss should an unfortunate event occur.

The point is that the promise of a financially worry-free retirement is becoming more and more a myth on the American social landscape. Proactively planning and developing viable backup plans should be a part of the repertoire of any prudent prospective retiree of moderate financial means. A significant part of this planning is likely to require the exercise of self-discipline and restraint on the level of consumption and material indulgence to which many of us lucky enough to live in affluent societies have become accustomed.

A financial pillar of our society is pensions. Having some means by which workers can exit the work force and remain financially solvent reduces society's economic costs of caring for the elderly and infirm. In recognition of this, most highly developed economies, such as the United States, have developed various pension systems to address this need.

References
1. Pension Benefit Guaranty Corporation, http://www.pbgc.gov/workers-retirees/about-pbgc/content/page1020.html.
2. Pension Benefit Guaranty Corporation, Performance and Accountability Report, Fiscal Year 2005.
3. Congressional Budget Office, The Risk Exposure of the Pension Benefit Guaranty Corporation, September 2005.
4. Government Accountability Office, Questions Regarding the Pension Benefit Guaranty Corporation's Practices Regarding Single-Employer Probable Claims, September 2005, GAO-05-991R.
5. Schroeder, Michael, Deficit Narrows at Pension Agency; Outlook Murky, Wall Street Journal, November 16, 2005.
6. Economist, The Print Edition, Corporate America's Legacy Costs: Now for the Reckoning, October 13, 2004.
7. Curry, Timothy, and Shibut, Lynn, The Cost of the Savings and Loan Crisis: Truth and Consequences, FDIC Banking Review, 2000.
8. Greenhouse, Steven, Transit Strike Reflects Nationwide Pension Woes, The New York Times, December 25, 2005.
9. Brewster, Deborah, Warning on U.S. State Pension Funds, Financial Times,
10. May 31, 2005.
11. Voice of San Diego, City of San Diego Financial Timeline, February 11, 2005.

CHAPTER FIVE
Healthcare and Demographics

A recent survey by the Kaiser Family Foundation, in June of 2005, reported that the top financial concerns for American adults are increasing health care cost. Americans are more concerned about having to pay more for health care then job loss or terrorism. Related health care concerns were:

- For those with health insurance, more than a third of the adults surveyed believed their health plan was more concerned with saving money than providing the best quality of care to them.

- More than one-third of Americans say they are very worried about not being able to afford their prescription drugs and the health care services they need.

- Three in ten adults are very worried about losing their insurance coverage, and that the quality of their health care is getting worse.

In general, women were more concerned than men about these issues. The researchers believe this is because women tend to be the health care decision makers in the home and tend to have lower incomes than men.

The evidence indicates this concern is well founded. The growth in health care cost in America has been staggering. In 1960, health care expenditures in the United States were $27 billion. By 1993 health care expenditures in the United States had grown to $888 billion, an average growth rate of more than 11% per year. One might argue that the American economy also grew during this period of time so the numbers are not as bad as they look. However, as a percentage of the economy, as measured by GDP (gross domestic product), in 1960, health care expenditures were about 5.1% of economy. By 1993 health care expenditures were about 13.3% of the economy. From 1993 to through 1999 health care expenses moderated and by 1999 national health care expenditures were about $1.2 trillion, or about 13.2% of the economy. Between 2000 and 2002 growth picked up again. By 2003 health care expenditures represented 15.3% of the economy. With a population of 296 million people in the United States, the average health care cost person was $5,670 per person in 2003.

As one might expect, national health care expenditures are a significant concern to the Federal government. As a result, they keep fairly comprehensive data on health care expenditures and routinely try to project what future national health care expenditures will be. Based upon economic and demographic assumptions found in the governments 2004 Medicare Trustees Report, and 2004 Old-Age and Survivors Insurance and Disability Insurance Trustees Report, national health care expenditures are expected to rise from $1.7 trillion in 2003 to $3.6 trillion in 2014. This includes the government's estimate of the effects associated with Medicare D, the prescription drug benefit now offered to Medicare recipients. The average rate of growth in national health care expenditures is expected to be 7.1% annually through 2014. By 2014 national health care spending is expected to be 18.7% of the economy.

National health care expenditures are comprised of private spending on health care as well as public spending. Public spending are health care expenditures paid by Federal, state, and local governments. Private health care spending includes expenditures paid for by individuals' out of pocket health care expenses and private health insurance, as well as health services provided in industrial settings. The "good" news is that private personal health care spending growth is expected to gradually slow from 8% in 2003 to around 5.9% in 2014. The bad news is that this slowing in growth is expected to be because of slower growth in personal income and an increase in the uninsured population. Health insurance premiums are expected to grow at about 6.6%. Because of efforts by employers and insurers to contain their costs, out-of-pocket spending for the individual is expected to grow more rapidly.

The Organization for Economic Cooperation and Development (OECD) is an organization comprised of the most advanced economies in the world, including the United States. Among its other functions, it collects comparative data on the healthcare systems of these countries. The United States spends more as a percentage of the economy than any other advanced economy and industrialized nation. In 2003, 15% of GDP was spent on health care in the United States. The average for the OECD countries was 8.6% with Switzerland and Germany spending around 11% and Canada and France spending around 10%. The United States also spends more per capita than any other advanced country. In 2003, the United States spent $5,635 per capita. This was more than twice the average of $2,307 per capita for the countries in the OECD.

If one were ethnocentrically inclined, it would be easy to succumb to the belief that even though the United States has the most expensive system, it is the best system. This may be an erroneous conclusion. The United States has fewer physicians per capita than most other OECD countries. In 2002, the United States had 2.3 physicians per 1000 population, as opposed to 2.9 practicing physicians as the average for OECD countries. There were 7.9 nurses per 1000 population, as opposed to 8.2 for the OECD countries. The number of acute hospital beds in the United States in 2003 was 2.8 per 1000 population with the OECD countries also being 2.8.

One measure of the quality of healthcare might be gains in life expectancy. In the United States, life expectancy increased from 1960-2002 by 7.3 years. In Japan, life expectancy increased by 14 years and in Canada by 8.4 years. In 2002/3, life expectancy in the United States was 77.2 years. The average for OECD countries was 77.8 years. Japan, Iceland, Spain, Switzerland, and Australia took the honors of the OECD countries with the highest life expectancies.

Infant mortality is also a measure of the quality of the healthcare a country offers its citizens. In the United States in 2002, infant mortality was 7 deaths per 1000 live births, which is above the OECD average of 6.1 deaths per live births. The countries with the lowest infant mortality rates were Iceland, Sweden, Finland, and Norway. They all had infant mortality rates below 3.5 deaths per 1000 live births.

When faced with information that you are paying more and getting less, it is prudent to ask what is going on. Paying more and getting less is a sign of economic inefficiency, especially when there is evidence that other countries' healthcare systems seem to be more cost effective. A clue to the answer of this question might be found in how healthcare is financed in various countries. One difference that stands out when looking at how healthcare is financed is that in all of the OECD countries, except for the United States, Mexico, and Korea, the public sector is the primary funding source. The public sector sources are governmental. The average share of funding for healthcare provided by the public sector is 72% of total funding. In the Nordic countries as Denmark, Norway, and Sweden, over 80% of total healthcare is funded by the public sector. In the United States, only 44% of total healthcare funding is funded by the public sector. Private insurance accounts for over 37% of total health spending in the United States. This is significantly larger than the role private insurance plays in any of the other OECD countries. Moreover, despite the highest total overall cost for healthcare of any advanced economy in the world, over 46 million people do not have any health insurance coverage.

In 2003, the Department of Health and Human Services produced its first National Healthcare Quality Report. The purpose of the report is to track the state of healthcare quality for the United States on annual basis. It is considered the most extensive ongoing examination of quality of healthcare ever undertaken in any major industrialized country, including the United States. The first report found that high quality of healthcare was not to be universally found in the United States. In particular, the report cited deficiencies in preventative care and the management of chronic diseases as missed opportunities for improvement. The second report, done in 2004, found some improvement, but also identified specific areas where major improvements could be made. In particular, it concluded that the "gap between the best possible care, and actual care remains large."

This is a situation that would seem to contradict the fundamental principles of free market economics. In a free market economic system, competition from rival service providers should deliver the best healthcare to the consumer at the lowest cost. The evidence we have reviewed says that the healthcare system in the United States delivers the highest cost healthcare, with less than the highest quality, and still leaves significant numbers of people without funding for healthcare. Why is it that many countries, with the major source of healthcare funding being the public sector, are able to deliver comparable, or better healthcare services to their citizens at significantly lower cost? The problem is that a true free market economic system has many buyers and many sellers. As a consequence, no one seller has enough individual economic power to shape the market to its agenda. As a consequence, real competition between two sellers can occur to the benefit of the consumer by efficiently allocating money and healthcare and to deliver the highest quality healthcare services at the lowest cost.

Despite the free market rhetoric, in the United States we do not have a real free market system for delivering healthcare services. Rather than many service providers, no one of whom has significant enough economic power to shape its market, we have what is called an oligarchic economic system with regard to healthcare. We have a smaller number of service providers who have concentrated their economic power sufficiently to shape the market for their services through political influence such as lobbying, massive amounts of capital poured into advertising to shape consumer preference, and huge amounts of money directed toward the physician gatekeepers of service delivery. This system has lead to a wasteful and inefficient use of money intended for healthcare. The consequences are unnecessary costs built into the system as a part of the economic landscape, and a social system overburdened with a need for services at ever increasing cost and ever diminishing means to pay. A recent example of this is a recent article in the Journal of the American Medical Society. Pharmaceutical companies represent a mega industry. Their economic power and reach extend into halls of Congress through paid lobbyists and into the rooms of practicing physicians. This article found that 90% of the $21 billion dollars the pharmaceutical companies spends on marketing goes directly to the physicians. A conclusion of this article is that this is a conflict of interest which can compromise the judgment of the physician in the recommendation, or delivery, of health care services to the patient.

The physicians receive these payments through small gifts, pharmaceutical samples, continuing medical education, funds for physician travel, speakers bureaus, ghostwriting, and consulting and research contracts. From a business and marketing viewpoint, for the pharmaceutical companies, this is an excellent strategy. The most effective use of marketing dollars should be directed towards influencing those individuals or organizations which can most influence purchasing decisions. From the public and individual healthcare consumer's point of view, however, this conflict of interest between the pharmaceutical companies and the physicians represents potentially higher costs and lower quality care. Even assuming an ethically conscientious physician, the current system is configured so that money buys access to the limited time and attention practicing physicians have available to sort through voluminous information about the comparative efficacy of different treatment alternatives. Unfortunately, we also know that not all physicians are as ethically conscientious as their professional commitments and standards represent.

The intent of this analysis is not to be critical of the medical and healthcare professions. These professions are an integrated part of our social and economic landscape. Our agenda is to establish a foundation that is representative of what is, so that we might better determine what is most likely to be in the future. While some components of the economic structure of our healthcare system will inevitably change, the basic structure is too massive, with too many entrenched and powerful interests, to change until a severe crisis mandates a massive structural change. With the demographics of millions of aging retiring baby boomers needing more healthcare services, corporations that have overextended their health insurances promises beyond what they can deliver and still remain competitive and Federal and State entitlement budgets stretched to the breaking point, we are staring at a severe crisis in providing access to quality healthcare at affordable costs. As such, it is reasonable to conclude that we will be looking at some type of massive structural change in our healthcare system.

Of particular interest is how this massive structural change might occur, what it might look like, and what the implications for its direct impact on our lives and our investments might be. In order to better explore the answers to these questions, we will turn our attention to two of the biggest players in this scene, the Medicare system and corporate healthcare benefits.

Behind Social Security, Medicare is the second largest social insurance program in the United States. It is intended to provide a baseline of healthcare for the county's aging and disabled citizens. In 2004, nearly forty-two million Americans were receiving benefits from Medicare. It has two components known as Hospital Insurance and Supplemental Medical Insurance. The Hospital Insurance component is commonly known as Part A of Medicare. It is a statutory entitlement to qualified sixty-five-year-old citizens. It is non-elective, and no insurance premiums are required to participate in Medicare Part A. Similar to Social Security, the Medicare Health Insurance Trust Fund is intended to accumulate funding for current and future Medicare Health Insurance beneficiaries. It is funded by Federal government tax revenues, which are based on the prescribed rate, set by law, and can only be changed by a law modifying that tax rate.

The Supplemental Medical Insurance component of Medicare must be elected by a prospective beneficiary in order to be covered. Coverage by Supplemental Medical Insurance, known as Parts B, and now the prescription drug plan, Part

D, require an additional insurance premium to be paid by the individual in order for coverage to occur. The premiums for Part D coverage can be readjusted each year based on the actual expense experienced by Medicare in offering this coverage. Medicare's Supplemental Medical Insurance also has a trust fund associated with its operating funding.

Much political and economic discussion has occurred regarding the dire funding circumstances of the Social Security program. Often the Social Security financial problem highlighted is fifty to seventy-five years into the future, when the system solvency may be threatened. The 2005 Report of the Trustees of the Medicare trust fund concludes that the solvency problem for the Medicare is already beginning. The real problem is with the Health Insurance Trust. The 2005 Medicare Trustees report says that the Health Insurance trust fund is not adequately financed over the next ten years. In 2004, for the first time since 1998, the Health Insurance Trust Fund was spending more than the funding it was receiving. The report concludes that the "fund assets are projected to be exhausted in 2020". In order to arrive at these conclusions, the trustees needed to make some economic assumptions about inflation and economic growth, among other things. The assumptions were what they called intermediate, which means somewhere between what was considered best case and worst case values for inflation and economic growth.

An overall conclusion reached by the Medicare trustees was that," The financial outlook for the Medicare program continues to raise serious concerns. Total Medicare expenditures were $309 billion in 2004 and are expected to increase in future years at a faster pace than either workers' earnings or the economy overall. As a percentage of GDP, expenditures are projected to increase from 2.6% currently to 13.6% by 2079, based upon our intermediate set of assumptions. Growth of this magnitude, if realized, would place a substantially greater strain on the nation's workers, Medicare beneficiaries, and the Federal Budget."

My own opinion is that the "intermediate" economic assumptions used in these projections are too optimistic. Interest rates are likely to be driven up by the need for greater and greater deficit funding for the Federal budget. This would likely have a dampening effect upon economic growth in the United States, which will additionally see increased costs for energy and raw materials. Greater demand from countries like China and India are likely to drive prices up creating greater inflationary pressure as well as slower economic growth. This is referred to as stagflation, the worst of all economic conditions. If these scenarios prove to be correct, the situation for Medicare and the nation's senior and disabled citizens is even grimmer than the Medicare trustees report concludes.

However, even if we accept the assumptions of their report, the conclusions are alarming. Within fourteen years the current Medicare system will be broke. The year 2006 is considered the year the first wave of baby boomers start to retire. Under the current Medicare system they are looking at approaching age eighty with an insolvent healthcare system to provide for their needs. Each successive year of retirees faces an even bleaker outlook for healthcare under the present Medicare system.

The situation with the financial soundness of the Medicare is urgent. No credible voice knowledgeable of Medicare's financial circumstances would disagree. The problem is what to do about it. Without advocating any particular solution, but merely to lay out the potential solutions for our consideration, only a few general approaches can be taken to address this pending healthcare crisis. Medicare benefits can be reduced or eliminated, greater efficiencies can be sought to reduce costs, and greater funding can be generated to pay for the system, or some combination of these approaches can be used. The likelihood of the effectiveness of any of these approaches making meaningful positive changes in the Medicare system appears dubious to me.

Let's consider these general approaches to solving this prospective healthcare crisis. Reducing or eliminating Medicare benefits for a growing population of needy senior and disabled citizens does not suggest itself as an approach that would lead to anything other than social upheaval and distress. Political obstacles would need to be overcome. It is reasonable to believe that advocacy organizations that serve as a political voice for groups that would be impacted by reduction or elimination of Medicare benefits would become quite active in opposition to any such attempt. Any politician campaigning on a platform of reducing or eliminating Medicare benefits would find rival opposition candidates more than willing accept the support of opposition groups. The increasing numbers of Medicare beneficiaries potentially affected by elimination or reduction of benefits would make them a powerful political force. The net result of this approach is likely to be a quagmire at best.

Increasing funding to pay for the Medicare system has primarily one source. It must come from increased taxes and/or premiums for Medicare coverage. Creating greater economic efficiencies in the operations of Medicare, and the healthcare system, in general, could provide a more cost effective delivery of services by creating a significant change in the medical and healthcare system. The problem with economic inefficiencies is that social resources such as healthcare are not as cost effectively delivered from the end users point of view. From the vendor's point of view, however, it is these system inefficiencies that provide the opportunity for more profitable business operations than might otherwise be encountered in a healthcare delivery environment driven by economic efficiency. This creates a status quo of vested interests of very well financed private interest groups whose voice is well heard among politicians seeking funding for their campaigns and their affiliated stakeholders.

The most recent example of a significant change in the Medicare system has been the passage into law and implementation of the Prescription Drug Plan, or Medicare Part D, which has created greater cost and poorer delivery of services. A recent article in public media cited the following problems occurring as a result of this new program:

- Some beneficiaries are being told they don't have coverage when they do. Others find that the drugs are covered but other needed supplies aren't.
- Some beneficiaries haven't received enrollment cards.
- Many with chronic conditions find that no plan covers all their medications.
- Wait times for information are long, and the information dispensed is not always correct. The Social Security Administration, which administers some aspects of the Medicare plan, says its help lines have been so overwhelmed that other services are beginning to suffer.
- Some are being overcharged dramatically, charged hundreds of dollars when they owe only a co-payment of $1 or $5.
- Some pharmacists have yet to be paid.
- California and Missouri have sued over a requirement that any savings accrued by state plans because of the Medicare changes be returned to the federal

government. Both say it's taking hundreds of millions of dollars away from those who need it most.

- Some plans require that beneficiaries switch to a particular pharmacy.

If this is a representative example of what operational reform Medicare would look like, it is not an encouraging sign. With the magnitude of the problem large and immediate, not a lot of time exists to be able to effectively address the problems, let alone recover from set backs.

The remaining possibility for addressing the looming Medicare healthcare funding crisis is to increase revenues for the Medicare system by raising the premiums paid for coverage or increasing payroll taxes. In either case, it means additional money coming in from current and future beneficiaries. The Heritage Foundation is a conservative think tank. Their mission is to "to formulate and promote conservative public policies based on the principles of free enterprise, limited government, individual freedom, traditional American values, and a strong national defense". In a study published by them towards the end of 2005, they looked at the economic effects financing Medicare's unfunded liabilities. They found that in order to adequately finance Medicare's current and future obligations, taxes would have to immediately increase from 2.9% to 13.4% of payrolls.

Although there is disagreement among economists concerning what effect increases in taxes have on the economy, they generally agree that there is an effect. A negative effective effect on economic growth is much more likely when tax increases are larger. An increase in taxes by the amount the Heritage Foundation found necessary could be considered a large increase. When we consider the rest of the financial woes of the Federal government, the impact is all the more severe, because other areas of government operations would also require additional funding. How negative an impact tax increases might have would depend on whether they were actually used to pay down debt, or whether they were used to finance higher government spending in other areas of the Federal budget. The Heritage Foundation study came to the conclusion that raising personal income and payroll taxes high enough to finance Medicare from 2005 through 2015 could cost over 800,000 jobs and slow economic growth by over $87 billion a year, on average. The longer term economic costs of adequately funded Medicare for the next seventy-five years are estimated to be at a cost of 2.7 million jobs and a decrease in economic growth of almost $248 billion over the first ten years that higher payroll taxes are in place.

Behaving in a financially responsible manner has not been held in high esteem by the American voter, other than rhetorically. Politicians in a democratic society have been all too willing to accommodate the financial excesses demanded by their constituencies. We have no reason to believe that we can expect any fundamental behavioral change which would make it more likely that Medicare will be adequately financed by the higher taxes necessary to assure its financial solvency. Moreover, even if such a change were to occur, the economic consequences would not be good for the American economy because of job losses and sluggish or recessionary economic growth.

The dire Medicare financial picture is only a part of the pending healthcare crisis for the United States. After the Second World War, offering health coverage to workers was one way they could get increased compensation in spite of existing wage controls. Offering health insurance coverage became institutionalized in many businesses. About 174 million Americans are covered by health insurance from their employer or their spouse's employer. This has become a variable cost of doing business for these firms and is an expense that affects a company's profitability. As the world economy has become more globalized, many of these firms now have to compete with firms from other countries that do not have to carry these legacy costs. With wages and benefits often being one of the most significant expenses that affect a company's competitiveness, many American companies cannot effectively compete with their foreign rivals. To compound the difficulty, healthcare costs increase each year while pricing pressure forces companies to be price competitive with their offerings. Something has got to give. That something is a general trend to reduce or eliminate healthcare benefits to current and retired workers. A variation of this is asking employees, and retirees to contribute more for their health insurance coverage. While a reasonable response, it does have economic consequences for the individual and society as a whole.

In a *New York Times* report on the difficulties people were having paying for their healthcare insurance, the newspaper said that companies are shifting more and more costs to consumers in the form of higher deductibles, co-payments, or premiums. As a consequence, with very low savings and carrying higher levels of personal debt, many Americans are put in financial distress because of these additional medical costs. This is true even for many people with insurance. Of the more than 1.5 million families who filed for bankruptcy in 2004, the most common causes were job loss and medical expenses. To quote from the *New York Times* report, "In a study of 1,771 people who filed for bankruptcy, reported this year by four researchers at Harvard and Ohio University, 28% said the cause was illness or injury. Most were middle class, educated and had health insurance at the start of treatment. Many lost phone service, went without meals or skipped medications to save money. Although the study relied largely on people's own accounts of their finances, the figure suggests that as many as 400,000 American families file for bankruptcy each year because of medical expenses."

While this may not be a full blown crisis unless you happen to be one of the unfortunate families who has had the direct experience of being thrown into financial distress because of medical and healthcare expenses, it looks to be a preview of the future for many, if not most, Americans. As we have seen from the earlier discussions on the funding of healthcare costs, the consumer is probably looking at less rather than more costs in this regard. A likely result will be a growing polarization between those individuals who are able to afford quality healthcare and the rest of the population.

The characteristic public policy response to serious social issues seems to be to placate the disenchanted until severe crisis conditions exist. At that point, it becomes politically expedient for policymakers to express public outrage that such conditions could exist, and advocate a vigorous political policy to address the problem. Before this occurs, however, we are likely to see growing numbers of Americans—working, retired, elderly, disabled, and impoverished—experience severe financial distress before their voices become loud enough to create a political response.

An aging population can be expected to have a higher need for healthcare. Even younger Americans appear to be declining in health. Reuter's news service reported in 2005 that the amount of money spent on treating obesity-related health problems soared tenfold between 1997 and 2002. By 2002, they reported that $36.5 billion per year was spent on obesity-linked medical issues. The larger scale consequence is that large numbers of impoverished Americans will be unable to obtain affordable healthcare, a circumstance which is likely to drag economic growth lower as the ability for discretionary spending deteriorates with personal economic circumstances. Higher levels of personal stress and desperation would contribute to the need for even greater healthcare access, making the situation deteriorate even further. We can expect growing social malaise and disorder with the breakup of families and relationships.

Our discussion, so far has assumed a continuation of the present state of affairs regarding healthcare. We have added no natural disasters or man-made disasters, such as war or terrorism. Were an unexpected event to occur which would place a great deal more demand upon the healthcare system, the costs would go up rapidly, as the quality and accessibility of services deteriorated. While it is difficult to factor this into consideration, our human experiences should tell us that sooner or later something unexpected happens, sometimes not for the better. Devastating earthquakes and storms are fairly unpredictable with regard to their occurrence and severity. The year 2005 saw a record number of severe hurricanes.

What is currently on the global radar, and is being watched by observers with increasing alarm, is a possible global influenza pandemic. An avian flu virus, known as H5N1, is spreading rapidly across the earth by migrating birds. It has made its way throughout Asia, Africa, and into Europe, with Germany, Greece and Italy being the latest to confirm its presence. While there is little evidence at the present time that it is spread from human to human, it has proven to be lethal when humans acquire it through handling infected birds. The concerns that the experts have, however, is that viruses are subject to change through mutation of their genetic structure. As the virus becomes more widespread and infects more humans, a strong possibility exists that the genetic structure of the H5N1 virus will come into contact with the human influenza virus. If sharing of genetic material occurred, the H5N1 virus could become transmissible from human to human. The recent emergence of this virus in Africa is of particular concern. The poor economies of the region make the virus more difficult to contain. In addition, this is a region where there is an already high incidence of human influenza. The likelihood of the mixing of the human and avian flu viruses is quite possible resulting in a variant that would be easily transmissible from human to human.

History has already given us a tragic example of a similar event. In 1918-1919 there was a "Spanish flu" that killed twenty-forty million people worldwide. Recent research indicates that flu virus probably originated from an avian flu that shared genetic material with human viruses. If we consider that the world population was significantly smaller in 1918 and that populations are much more mobile today, the deaths and impact of a similar pandemic today could be much more severe. Some estimates have the potential deaths from such a pandemic at over 150 million people. The economic costs are estimated in hundreds of billions of dollars. The global healthcare system including that of the United States is currently prepared to effectively cope with such a catastrophe.

What would a politically acceptable response be to a severe social healthcare crisis? We have had the opportunity to witness government responses to the excesses of corporate malfeasances, natural disasters, global political and military challenges, and the rebuilding of the American competitive and educational infrastructure. It would be challenging to find one result that could be said to have been definitively improved. From the opposite direction, there is evidence that we have spent a great deal of money and have received dubious value in return. The likely response to addressing an American healthcare crisis would be a backlash of letting free market economics sort out the healthcare issues through competition, as evidenced by Medicare's prescription drug program. We will likely see increased regulatory scrutiny of the healthcare establishment in a political attempt at making it the scapegoat for America's healthcare system ills.

Many say that the healthcare sector offers attractive investment prospects, because the demographics of an aging population will increase demand for services. I tend to take exception to this viewpoint, because it is difficult for me to believe that a likely increase in the regulatory environment and political pressure to contain pricing would be profitable for any business sector. Social and political considerations suggest it is more likely that the American healthcare system will be forced into a single payer type of model. In short, while this may seem heretical and outside the frame of reference of many observers, I believe the government will be forced into the nationalization of the healthcare system.

When, and if, this were to occur, observing some other countries that have adopted similar systems suggest the possibility that a two-tiered healthcare system will evolve. One system will be for people who require the services of the public healthcare system, and one for people who can afford to pay for private services. Any major structural realignment in the healthcare industry in the United States would likely cause a great deal of industry turmoil. It is impossible to know what the business and financial conditions of the healthcare related companies would be when the system stabilized. One thing that does appear likely, however, is that turmoil with regard to the investment characteristics of these companies will result. This will likely cause a great deal of volatility in company's stock share prices. A general sentiment of viewing healthcare companies as stalwarts of a sound investment program is probably unwarranted. Careful selection of companies having a definitive competitive advantage with regard to a niche sector or specialization area in high demand may prove fruitful.

References

1. Warner, Jennifer, Health Care Costs Top Worries, CBSNews.com, June 29, 2005.

2. Hoffman, Earl Dirk, Jr., et. al., Brief Summaries of Medicare & Medicaid, Title XVII and Title XIX of the Social Security Act, Centers for Medicare and Medicaid Services, Office of the Actuary, Department of Health and Human Services, November 1, 2005.

3. Desperate Measures: America's Healthcare Crisis, The Economist, January 26th, 2006.

4. OECD Health Data, 2005, www.oed.org.

5. 2004 National Healthcare Quality Report, Agency for Healthcare Research and Quality, United States Department of Health and Human Services, AHRQ Publication No. 05-0013, December 2004.

6. Brennan, Troyen A., et. al., Health Industry Practices That Create Conflicts of Interest, Journal of the American Medical Society, Vol. 295, No. 4, January 25, 2006, 429-433.

7. Warner, Margaret, Health Experts Urge Ban on Drug Company Gifts to Doctors, PBS interview with Dr. David Blumenthal, director of the Institute of Health Policy at Massachusetts General Hospital and professor at Harvard Medical School, http://www.pbs.org/newshour/health/, January 25, 2006.

8. The 2005 Annual Report Of The Boards Of Trustees Of The Federal Hospital Insurance And Federal Supplementary Medical Insurance Trust Funds, Submitted to Congress March 23, 2005.

9. Vrana, Deborah, Medicare's Drug Plan Mess, MSN

Money, http://moneycentral.msn.com/content/
Insurance/Insureyourhealth/P143247.asp., February
10, 2006.

10. Over The Fiscal Brink, Facing Facts, The Truth about Entitlements and the Budget, A Fax Alert from the Concord Coalition, Volume IX, Number 7- November 21, 2003.

11. Foertsch, Tracy L, and Joseph R. Antos, The Economic and Fiscal Effects of Financing Medicare's Unfunded Liabilities, The Heritage Foundation, www.heritage. org, October 11, 2005.

12. America's Healthcare Crisis; Desperate Measures, The Economist, January 26, 2006.

13. Leland, John, When Health Insurance Is Not Safeguarded, New York Times, October 23, 2005.

14. Dixon, Kim, Obesity costs soar tenfold to $36.5 billion in U.S., Reuters, June 27, 2005.

15. Lazzari, Stefano, and KlaU.S. Stohr, Avian influenza and influenza pandemics, Bulletin of the World Health Organization, April 2004, 82(4).

CHAPTER SIX
The Energy Situation

Overview

Everywhere I turn I see the footprint of petroleum. For example, the computer I am using is made of plastics and metals. Petroleum or natural gas is processed to provide the building blocks for various types of plastics. Aside from making up the components of electronic items, petroleum and natural gas also find their way into our lives through automotive components, major appliances, and the building and construction industry. Once these items are manufactured, communications systems, marketing, distribution, and transport systems serve roles to get them into our hands. At every step along the way, petroleum is either directly or indirectly involved in the process. I believe it is impossible to separate ourselves from the presence of petroleum in our lives.

I live in Oregon and enjoy the pristine beauty of nature and the wilderness. Even in the mountains and deep rain forests far removed from the developments of mankind, the evidence of petroleum's presence is abundantly found, from the clothing and equipment I bring with me to the method of transportation that got me at least partially there, to the jets, or satellites flying overhead, to the fertilizer that may have been used in the production of any food I brought with me. The presence of petroleum is everywhere. Our world's civilizations, and life as we have known it, have been built on the foundation of readily available and inexpensive access to the energy provided by the hydrocarbons found in petroleum. We are dependent on some source of energy for survival and commerce. At the present time petroleum is the lifeline of our existence.

The problem is that there is a finite amount of petroleum.

This is our potential supply. Although petroleum has been used for ages by mankind since its discovery by Drake in 1859 in Titusville, Pennsylvania, the rate of consumption has increased sharply. Since no more petroleum is being made, a time will come when the existing supply of petroleum is depleted. However, depletion is not an all or nothing idea. It does not mean that we will get up one morning and find there is no longer any oil. There are various stages of depletion ranging from 0% to 100%. The more rapidly we consume the existing supplies of petroleum, the more rapidly we move from 0% to 100% depletion. The real question that should concern us is what will be the direct impact of various stages of petroleum depletion on our personal lives.

A preview of what we might be looking at can be seen by observing the current price of oil. As of this writing, oil has been trading at $55 to $60 a barrel for several weeks. Oil and gasoline prices have become mainstream media issues. My older son, who lives in Northern California, recently reported to me that gasoline in his area costs around $3.00 per gallon. A fifteen gallon tank would cost $45 to fill up. For a fifteen mile per gallon vehicle with moderate usage, a tank a week would be $200 per month for fuel costs alone. Adding in insurance and maintenance of $100 to $150 per month puts the operating costs of a vehicle at $300 to $350 per month, not including possible vehicle payments. Factor in the potential costs of purchasing another car to be $100 to $200 per month, and we are estimate vehicle operating costs of $400 to $500 per month. This estimate is consistent with a 2005 study of vehicle operating costs which found the range to be from $400 to $1,200 per month depending upon the vehicle. The United

States Bureau of Labor Statistics reports that the average annual wage in the United States in 2002 was $36,764 per year. This is just under $3,100 per month or assuming 35% for various taxes, about $2,000 per month after taxes. The low end of our operating cost estimate represents 25% of an individual's annual wage going to cover the expenses of operating a vehicle. The price of gasoline represents only one component of the increased personal expenses from increased oil prices. A recent Wall Street Journal article summarized this predicament fairly well as it stated:

"Mr. Bellini, a 51-year-old line technician for Comcast Corp., hasn't received a pay increase in three years, since 2002. His wages have been stuck at $19.10 an hour while overall consumer prices have risen 8%. Since then, however, the cost of many necessities has soared well beyond the averages. As of June, for example, the price of gasoline had risen 55%, and bread and meat rose 10% and 18%, respectively. Milk prices jumped 14% and electricity 11%.

Despite an economy growing at roughly 4%, healthy corporate profits and low unemployment levels, annual wages of workers in non-managerial positions—representing about 80% of the U.S. work force—rose 2.7% in June from a year ago, according to the Bureau of Labor Statistics. But adjusted for inflation, which cooled in June as gasoline prices declined, those wages were unchanged from a year ago. Annual wage growth hasn't outpaced inflation for 14 months."

As we have seen, relatively easy and inexpensive access to petroleum has been the one of the cornerstones upon which society and civilization, as we have known it, has developed. Increased oil costs will inevitably carry through to increased costs for everything, including home heating and cooling, clothing, building materials, food, and prescription medications.

Supply Side

Peak Oil

How long will the existing supplies of oil last? While no credible commentator would suggest an unlimited supply of oil, opinions differ significantly concerning when we will reach what is called peak oil. Peak oil, also known as Hubbert's Peak, after the late geophysicist, Dr. M. King Hubbert, is the idea that there will come a time after which the production of oil will continue to decline. In 1956, Hubbert predicted that U.S. oil production would peak in 1970 and decline from then on. His viewpoint was at variance with the popularly accepted dogma at that time, and Hubbert was not taken seriously. However, his analysis has since proved to be remarkably accurate. In fact, the United States did reach its peak of domestic oil production in 1970, and it has declined since then. This is now an established fact and can be verified through the American Petroleum Institute's statistical database.

Proven Oil Reserves is a concept measuring the amount of oil that can be recovered with reasonable certainty under existing economic and operating conditions. From the end of 1984 through the end of 2003, the Proven Oil Reserves of the United States declined by 39%. By the end of 2004, with current rates of production, this would give the United States twelve years before complete depletion of its Proven Oil Reserves. The United States is now dependent upon being able to import over 50% of its oil needs. The evidence suggests that the United States will become more dependent upon being able to import adequate oil supplies, rather than less dependent.

It is important to recognize the implications of this situation for any personal financial planning or investment strategy. The oil situation represents a likely pending crisis. As with most crises, there are both risks and opportunities. A major risk would be to be financially unprepared for an event that could be of monumental consequence in its impact on our lives. While no one has a crystal ball for the future, there are times when the structural facts of a circumstance increase the probability that an event will occur, sometimes significantly. Failing to prepare for a highly probable, or probable, adverse event is an invitation to disaster. The other side of the coin is to recognize the opportunities presented by a probable event. In this situation, it is the recognition of the opportunities, presented by the oil and energy situation, which also hold a key to adequate preparation for its likely future outcome.

Since it has been established that the United States has already reached its peak of oil production, the next obvious question is what about the oil production peak for the rest of the world. Opinions on when the global oil production peak will occur vary. The estimates range from it has already occurred within the last several years to twenty-five to thirty years from now.

When this point is reached, we can expect decreasing supplies oil. When this time is reached, if oil is still our primary energy source, we can expect to pay ever higher prices for everything from fuel, to food, and medicine. This would be a driver for price inflation. High oil prices have also been associated with slowed economic growth. The additional cost of oil acts like a tax and siphons off money which could be spent on consumer goods or business investment. Consumer purchasing and business investment are two major sources of economic growth. If economic growth slows enough, it becomes an economic recession, or in severe cases, an economic depression. Because businesses have difficult times earning money when a recession or depression occurs, unemployment increases as a result of employee layoffs from business trying to cut their operating costs. Unless there is some kind of stimuli, like government intervention, to get the economy going again, economic conditions deteriorate until marginal and weak businesses are eliminated. Some would argue that if this were to occur, it would leave a stronger economic system behind. While there might be some merit to this argument from a larger societal perspective, from the individual and family perspective the personal human costs would likely be distressing and painful. As families and individuals with limited public policy making power, it would be good planning to be as prepared for this type of economic disruption.

North America

The United States is in the declining phase of its production cycle. Given the evidence of the past thirty-five years, the United States will experience significant decreases its production of oil. Annual oil production is likely to continue to decrease.

Canada is still relatively rich in resources and will be a continuing supplemental source of imported oil to the U.S. As the price of oil increases and the technology improves, alternative sources of oil which were once considered economically unfeasible will become potential sources of oil. The Athabasca Tar Sands is one example of a North American alternative petroleum resource.

Latin America

Mexico is a potential source of oil south of the U.S. border. The major Mexican oil production site is the Cantarell Field. This is the world's second production site, after Ghawar in Saudi Arabia. On August 2, 2006, Bloomberg news reported the state-owned oil monopoly Petroleos Mexicanos said production would decline by 8% in 2006. These production declines are expected to continue. Mexico is one of the top three suppliers of oil to the United States.

Brazil and Venezuela are the significant oil producers in South America. Venezuela produces the lion's share of South American oil. Venezuela has been one of the significant sources of non-Mideast oil to the U.S. The problem now is that political differences between the U.S. and Venezuelan governments may jeopardize Venezuela as a significant source of oil to the U.S. Bolivia and Ecuador, two other sources of Latin American carbon based energy have both started expressing an intent to nationalize their fields.

Saudi Arabia

Saudi Arabia is considered to have the only real excess oil production capacity at present. Even if they do, by their own recent statements they have concerns whether or not they will have adequate oil to meet global needs. A recent published work by Matthew Simmons, an oil industry expert with more than thirty years of experience, has called into question whether Saudi Arabia really does have as much oil reserves as it claims. In his detailed, expert, and well documented analysis, he comes to the conclusion that Saudi Arabia's estimated reserves are significantly overstated. Even if the Saudi's were willing to continue their efforts at stabilizing the supply of oil, they may not have the capacity to do so. In fact, the Financial Times reported that senior Saudi energy officials warned their U.S. and European counterparts that OPEC would have an extremely difficult time meeting the oil needs of the world. Saudi Arabia estimates a 4.5m barrel/day gap between what the world needs and what they can supply.

An additional concern is the political stability of Saudi Arabia. The Saudi social system is stratified with the petroleum oligarchs and their supporting systems as the primary beneficiaries of Saudi political power of wealth. There are vast numbers of other Saudi citizens who have not been uplifted by Saudi Arabia's vast oil wealth. According to the CIA Factbook, Saudi Arabia's 2004 unemployment rate was over 25%. Over half the population is under age twenty-one, and the literacy rate, the percent of population over age fifteen who can read, is close to 80%. This large segment of impoverished, disenfranchised and literate young Saudis is one reason why Saudi Arabia is a hotbed of radical Islam. This core of radical Islam is a challenge to the existing Saudi regime and presents at least a reasonable possibility of political turmoil, if not outright disruption of the existing Saudi regime. The Middle East has over 60% of the world's petroleum reserves. The potential political instability of the Middle East region and Saudi Arabia, in particular, makes the security of the world's petroleum reserves truly built on a foundation of shifting sands.

Russia

The world's eighth largest proven oil reserves, the second largest coal reserves, and the largest natural gas reserves are found in Russia. In 2003 Russia was the world's second largest exporter of oil behind Saudi Arabia, and for part of 2004, Russian exports of oil actually were higher than those of Saudi Arabia. While experts believe Russian oil production will continue to grow in the short term, most of Russia's proven reserves are in Siberia. Oil productivity increased from 1999 through 2004. While in the hands of private ownership and operators, there was incentive to increase productivity by applying more advanced extraction methods to Russia's aging oil fields. The effective nationalization of the Russian oil giant Yuko, has appeared to have caused a chill in the productivity improvements needed to continue increasing oil production. In addition, a report from the Siberian branch of the Russian Academy of Science maintains that the proven reserves in Western Siberia are nearly 60% depleted. The greater the depletion, the more difficult and costly it becomes to extract the remaining reserves. Additionally, one must consider the strategic agenda of Russia's policy makers. The Russian economy needed the strong boost provided by increasing oil exports and the foreign currency reserves, primarily U.S. dollars that came along with it. Russia has established an economic stabilization fund that has accumulated close to $17 billion dollars. Russia does not want to see its economy dependent upon oil exports. They will likely use their accumulated oil wealth to diversify the strength of their economy. To the extent they are successful with weaning themselves off oil exports for the economic growth needed for a healthy economy, oil exports could then become a strategic card in negotiating global economic and political policy issues with oil needy countries such as the United States.

Caspian Sea

The Caspian Sea Region is another region of the world which, although having nowhere close to the oil reserves of the Middle East, holds significant reserves of oil. It comprises Azerbaijan, Kazakhstan, Turkmenistan, and the southern most parts of Russia, as well as Iran. Uzbekistan, while not directly on the Caspian Sea, is also included as the region's largest natural gas producer. The Caspian Sea region holds the third largest oil and gas reserves, behind the Middle East and Russia. Here, as in the Middle East, geopolitical factors constrain the fuller development and distribution of these oil and gas reserves to the rest of the world. In general, the countries of this region are very poor. The break-up of the Soviet Union caused economic turmoil as regional trade collapsed. The latter half of the 1990's has seen some economic improvements. However, poorly developed infrastructure from underinvestment, a general lack of agreement on the division of the Caspian Sea's oil and gas resources, regional conflicts arising from the numerous religious and ethnic groups of the region, and serious environmental issues from years of neglect and mismanagement present difficult obstacles to the development of the oil and gas resources of the Caspian Sea region. Moreover, even if these obstacles were not present, the potential supply available to meet the world's projected energy needs is a fairly modest four million barrels per day production level by the year 2015.

Other

Even if we make the doubtful, but optimistic assumption, that reserves of oil will be adequate to supply global demand in the coming years, serious issues with regard to the supply and distribution chains that process crude oil and get it to markets exist. The significant reserves of oil are located in countries, or regions, that either are not particularly friendly to U.S. interests, or are politically unstable. We have already discussed the political fragility of Middle East oil supplies. In addition, the second most prominent supplier of oil, Russia, has declining reserves and a strategically politically savvy leadership which, judging from past history, would not hesitate to use the leverage of its oil reserves to further its own political agendas. Other significant sources of oil are from South America, with Venezuela of particular importance. Unfortunately, the current leadership of Venezuela is not favorably predisposed to the United States, and in the face of increasing demand from

China and India may divert more of its production to places other than the United States.

Distribution

While the primary global sources of oil highlight the political fragility of the oil supply chain, bringing the oil to market is done through systems of pipelines, oil tankers, and trucks that have to get the crude oil to the refineries to be processed into the multitude of products it becomes, with gasoline as one of the most common end products. The pipelines present their own unique set of problems. In areas such as the Caspian Sea region, getting the crude oil to ports where it can be loaded on to tankers to be delivered to refineries will require the construction of a network of pipelines through several different independent countries of the former Soviet Union. Ethnic, cultural, and political differences may delay or interrupt the building or operation of these pipelines. The routes of new pipelines are also an issue that is the subject of intense geopolitical strategy maneuvers. The United States is competing with other countries and economies also dependent upon imported oil. China and India are two heavyweight powers that need to be reckoned with. They each have enormous energy needs, and especially in the case of China, they are acquiring the economic muscle to be extremely capable competitors in the quest for oil. The placement of pipeline routes to shipping ports in locations that favor transport to these countries creates an advantage with regard to access and control of oil resources. Moreover, with pipeline routes through countries which are favorably predisposed to an agenda, the fact they are more easily influenced or controlled can be a strategic advantage. The inherent importance of oil to civilization makes it a strategic commodity. It is naïve to neglect to consider how the geopolitical factors will play out regarding access and control of oil resources when considering how the economic and investment environment will impact one's personal financial circumstances.

Refinery Capacity Limitations

Oil supply is not the only issue that needs to be addressed when considering global energy and the impact on the economy, investment environments, and one's personal financial circumstances. A primary product of oil is gasoline. This means that crude oil must be processed at a refinery to produce gasoline. Aside from the availability of crude oil to process into gasoline, there must be adequate refinery capacity to process sufficient amounts of crude oil into gasoline. The United States has not had a new refinery built in thirty years. Refineries are working at capacity. Even if oil supplies were adequate, the ability to produce significantly higher quantities of gasoline is limited.

Under-investment in refinery infrastructure over the last thirty years means refineries are operating at or near capacity with aging and inefficient equipment. In the last several years we have witnessed serious explosions at several U.S. refineries. As I am writing this, Hurricane Katrina has just devastated the Gulf Coast of the United States. This has shut down many refineries and crude oil production operations. The initial projections as a result of this supply disruption are for gasoline price spikes. When operating at capacity with a limited resource, any disruption in the supply chain can have serious economic consequences. At the very least, the uncertainty of how, when, and the seriousness of a disruption will increase the investment risk. The uncertainty also increases the opportunity for gain through correctly understanding the economic implications of events associated with this resource. The greater one's understanding about what the adverse events and their consequences might be provides an important framework for personal financial and investment decision making.

Supply Disruptions

We have looked at how depleted oil supply reserves, problematic oil pipeline and distribution issues, and natural disasters such as Hurricane Katrina's impact on the U.S. Gulf Coast can cause serious disruptions in the global oil supply chain. These disruptions can have far-reaching economic consequences. One of the most obvious is increasing prices for gasoline or even rationing of gasoline. A direct effect of increased gasoline costs, especially in a personal use car dependent country such as the United States, is the additional money going to purchase gasoline, which means the money won't be available for other consumer purchases. In the United States, approximately two-thirds of economic growth is driven by consumer purchases. When consumers reduce their purchases, economic growth slows. Slowing economic growth may result in a recession, or in severe cases, a depression. In a recession, there is usually downward pressure on consumer prices. If businesses wish to sell products or services during an economic slowdown, they must make their offerings more affordable, because people have less money to spend. This may be more feasible for the business since its operating costs may also be lower because its ability to pay reduced wages in an environment of high unemployment. However, in the case of a limited resource with growing global demand, such as oil, prices may continue to increase, because a basic factor of production, upon which all else depends, continues to increase. The situation in which prices continue to increase during an economic slowdown is referred to a stagflation, stagnant economic growth and inflation, the worst combination of economic circumstances.

Demand Side

So far we have looked at oil from the perspective of supply limitations. In order to see a more complete picture we must look at the global need. In economic terms this is referred to as the demand for this resource. A simple and intuitively acceptable economic relationship is that of the relationship between supply, demand, and price. The basic idea is that the greater the demand for a product, and the more limited the supply, the more precious that product becomes, and consequently the higher the price that can be charged for it.

With regard to oil, the fact is that the global supply is, as we have discussed, finite. If global oil demand was slowing because of meaningful development of alternative energy sources, or reduced demand from global economies, the impact of a potentially reduced global supply of oil would be lessened. Unfortunately the opposite is occurring. Global oil demand is increasing, and is projected to continue to increase. While there is news of developing energy alternatives to oil, such as hybrid cars, solar energy, hydrogen fuel cells, etc., there is no unified and systematic program to make development of alternatives to oil a global or even national priority. Realistically, even if such a program were to be put on the table today, it would take ten to fifteen years to develop the technology, infrastructure, and commercial viability to the point of an operationally feasible alternative to oil. However, no such plan is available. Considering the complexity of political and business negotiations, let alone the technological development that would need to occur for such a program, the prospect of a plan appears to me to be many years into the future. I expect that a comprehensive and viable global or national energy plan is at least fifteen to twenty-five years into the future. As the impact of Hurricane Katrina all too tragically illustrates, ongoing energy crises of epic proportions are likely to play havoc with the global economic and investment environments. Those individuals and institutions who do not adequately factor in the impact of these energy crises may suffer devastating economic losses. However, those individuals who recognize how precious energy resources are likely to become and make sure they own a piece of the energy pie are likely to be well rewarded in the future.

United States

As with all people of the world, China's population of 1.3 billion people wants the material standard of living that the west has enjoyed for most of the twentieth century. Decades of the imposition of Communist ideology may have bottled up the entrepreneurial spirit of the Chinese people, but it did not kill it. The world is now witnessing the emergence of that economic force, which has already created a profound shift in the economic balance of power that has permanently transformed the economic world we have known. While there is no shortage of opinions as to what the consequences of this transformation will be and where if will go, one thing appears very clear. China's rapidly growing economy has an immense need for energy in order to continue its economic growth. BP is one of the world's largest gas and energy companies. Every year, for the last fifty years, BP compiles a Statistical Review of World Energy. This report is intended to provide an objective statement of the world energy picture. According to BP's 2004 report, China increased its consumption of oil from 2003 to 2004 by 15.8%. This represents almost a million barrel a day increase in consumption. On a global scale the global production of oil in 2004 was about 80,026,000 million barrels of oil per day. Global consumption for this same period was 80,757,000 million barrels of oil per day.

The ability to increase daily oil production seems to be approaching its limit. Saudi Arabia is looked to as the only remaining oil producer with the ability to increase daily production capacity. Saudi Arabia has expressed to desire and willingness to increase capacity if needed. This may be nothing more than political posturing. Oil industry expert, Matthew Simmon's well researched and thoroughly documented book Twilight in the Desert calls into question the ability of Saudi Arabia, which has provided no evidence to counter Simmon's claim, that Saudi oil reserves are highly overstated, as is their ability to increase daily production. In fact, Saudi officials have recently warned that Saudi Arabia may not be able to meet additional global oil demand. These circumstances certainly present a serious potential problem. In the words of a recent *Wall Street Journal* article in response to Hurricane Katrina's disruption of oil production in the U.S. Gulf region, "Western oil companies are already pumping at full capacity. Russia, the world's No. 2 producer, is producing all it can. Even Saudi Arabia, the top exporter, and its fellow members of the Organization of Petroleum Exporting Countries can do little to alleviate the emerging crisis. OPEC has spare capacity of some 1.5 million barrels a day." The world appears close to, or at, its production oil production capacity, and demand for additional oil is still growing, even by consideration of China's oil needs alone."

Some economic experts believe that China cannot sustain the phenomenal rate of economic growth is has experienced since the year 2000. While it remains to be seen what rate of economic growth is sustainable by China, little evidence exists that suggests China's economic growth will stop. The consequences of one hundred million additional oil consuming cars on the road is daunting when considering the limitations on the amount of oil that can be supplied over future years.

Moreover, China is not the only rapidly growing economic region with a rapidly growing demand for oil. The Energy Information Administration (EIA) of the U.S. Department of Energy identifies South Asia as comprised of the countries Bangladesh, Bhutan, India, the Maldives, Nepal, Pakistan, and Sri Lanka. The population of this region is an additional 1.4 billion people, or one-fifth of all the people in the world. Because of this region's past lagging economic growth, they have not been a relatively large consumer of energy, and oil in particular. That is changing. South Asia is emerging as a rapidly growing economic region. The EIA estimates that South Asia's oil imports will more than double by 2020, with the majority of those imports coming from the Middle East.

Supply Disruptions

The EIA recognizes the vulnerability of the global oil supply in its report on what it calls, World Oil Transit Chokepoints. This refers to the fact that about forty-three million barrels per day of oil pass by oil tanker through the narrow channels of waterways such as the Strait of Hormuz, which leads out of the Persian Gulf, and the Strait of Malacca which serves as a transport route for oil coming out of the middle east and heading toward consuming markets in Asia. These channels are very narrow and could be blocked by a natural disaster, an accident, or a deliberate act of sabotage. The EIA identifies at least seven of these strategic chokepoints. Shipping through these areas is also subject to pirate attacks. The International Chamber of Commerce's International Maritime Bureau's 2004 Annual Report on Piracy states that "Pirates preying on shipping were more violent than ever in 2004 and murdered a total of 30 crew members, compared with 21 in 2003". The highest number of attacks was in Indonesian waters. These chokepoints also represent a target of opportunity for terrorists wishing to disrupt the global economy through strategic attacks on the oil supply.

Alternatives

Given the possibility that the world may rapidly be approaching the peak of its available oil supply, and given that modern civilization is dependent upon an abundant, convenient, and economical source of energy, a prudent planning response would be to consider the alternatives should oil really arrive at the peak of its supply. While there are many alternative sources of energy, the development of either its commercial and/or technological feasibility for large scale use has not approached the stage of development where it could serve as a substitute for oil. Expert estimates are that it could realistically take decades before viable alternatives could be developed.

Some commonly viewed alternatives are natural gas, extraction of oil from Canadian oil sands, renewed interest in nuclear energy, solar energy, and hydrogen fuel cells. A basic and intuitive concept of economics is that of substitution. The idea of substitution is that as something becomes more and more expensive, consumers will substitute things that might be comparable in its place. While the current alternatives to oil may not be adequate to prevent serious disruption in the global economic system, they are important because they represent an emerging opportunity amidst a potential future crisis.

Investment Implications

The significance of a potential global energy crisis and its potential impact on your personal financial future cannot be overstated. Minimizing its importance as a potential opportunity or as a potential risk may be the difference between night and day with respect to planning your future. One method of planning for the future is to look at different future scenarios. Since there are an infinite number of these scenarios that might occur, we have to try to make an informed decision of what might be a plausible one. The prospect of a global energy crisis is a potential scenario. As a planning exercise that may illuminate where potential investment opportunities and hazards may be, let's weave a picture, using some creative fiction, of a potential future.

The headlines read "Manufacturers Ready to Pass on Costs". Over the last several years, businesses had absorbed the cost increases in their supplies and raw materials needed to operate. They had been having a difficult enough time competing for business with lower cost producers in China and India where labor costs were a fraction of what they were in the U.S. Since they had been able to keep their wage costs down because of an abundance of U.S. workers seeking work, they had still been able to eke out a declining but small profit. But now that oil prices have increased by 40% over the last year has driven gasoline prices higher, as well as the cost of everything else. Workers are demanding pay increases, and the costs of raw materials have skyrocketed. The shipping charges for the materials alone have eroded whatever little profit they were making. The only choice these companies had left was to raise their prices or go out of business. Besides, China and India now had the same problem. Business there also had to raise their prices, because their operating costs were also increasing. The oil shortage was not only a problem of the United States; it was also a global problem. Unfortunately, this meant that consumers all over the world, the United States in particular, had to pay more for everything. Since their costs of living had been increasing, consumers could no longer afford to work for the same incomes. They need increased incomes to pay for the necessities of housing, food, transportation, and health care. However, the price increases many businesses needed pushed them to the point where their products were not competitive. Many of these businesses had to close up shop. This meant that their former employees, many of whom were poorly prepared for unemployment, had to seek work. Besides the huge mortgages they had from the continual refinancing of their homes, they had additional credit card debt they had accumulated. They also had very little in savings for the proverbial rainy day fund. The problem was that employees from other businesses were also being laid off so it was not so easy to find other gainful employment. This turned into a vicious downward spiral. Increased unemployment meant fewer consumers able to purchase goods and services from business, which turned into a serious economic recession. Prices, however, which normally come down in a recession, were not coming down this time. The cost of oil, as a primary energy source, was still increasing because of the increasingly depleted supplies. This increased oil cost had to be passed on to whomever needed anything associated with oil, which essentially meant everything from gasoline, heating oil, clothing, pharmaceuticals, building materials, fertilizers for farming, and food.

References

1. http://motoring.racv.com.au/racvm/whichcar/
   CarreportArticle.cfm?ID=BA7BFA78-E832-4D45-
   A029ECDB1221A133

2. http://www.bls.gov/ro9/aapca.htm

3. Wall Street Journal, With Wages Flat a Family
   Struggles to Make Ends Meet; Why the Chevy Stays
   Parked, Kris Maher, Tuesday, July 19, 2005, page
   B1.

4. Nuclear Energy and the Fossil Fuels by M. King
   Hubbert, Chief Consultant (General Geology),
   Exploration and Production Research Division, Shell
   Development Company, Publication Number 95,
   Houston, Texas, June 1956, Presented before the
   Spring Meeting of the Southern District, American
   Petroleum Institute, Plaza Hotel, San Antonio, Texas,
   March 7-8-9, 1956.

5. Hatfield, Craig B., How Long Can Oil Supply Grow,
   Hubbert Center Newsletter #97/4, M. King Hubbert
   Center For Petroleum Supply Studies, Petroleum
   Engineering Department, Colorado School of Mines,
   October 1997, page1.

6. BP Statistical Review of World Energy, June 2005.

7. Hoyos, Carola, and Dennis, Neil, Saudis Warn of
   Shortfalls as Oil Hits $61, Financial Times, July 7,
   2005.

8. The World Factbook, www.cia.gov/cia/publications/
   factbook/geos/sa.html#Intro, August 22, 2005.

9. United States Department of Energy, Energy

Information Agency website, www.eia.doe.gov/emeu/
cabs/rU.S.sia.html, Current as of February 2005.

10. United States Department of Energy, Energy
Information Agency website, www.eia.doe.gov/emeu/
cabs/caspian.html#caspconf, Current as of December
2004.

11. BP 2004 Statistical Review of World Energy, June
2005.

12. Gold, Russell in Austin, Texas, and Herrick,
Thaddeus., Hurricane Raises Potential For a Global
Energy Crisis, Wall Street Journal, September 4,
2005.

13. http://www.eia.doe.gov/emeu/cabs/sasia.html,
website of the Energy Information Administration.
http://www.eia.doe.gov/cabs/choke.html, website of
the Energy Information Administration.

14. http://www.icc-ccs.org/main/news.php?newsid=40,
International Chamber of Commerce.

15. Mudevea, Anna, World Running Out of Time for
Oil Alternatives, Reuters / UK, August 18, 2005.

16. Black, Thomas, Pemex Says Cantarell 2006 Production
to Decline 8%, Bloomberg News, Bloomberg.com.

17. Lyons, John, Mexico's Biggest Oil Field Sees Decline,
The Wall Street Journal, August 2, 2006.

CHAPTER SEVEN
Geopolitics and Terrorism

It was just the crack of a grey dawn morning in Eugene, Oregon. I had been meeting my running buddy at 6:00 A.M. for years, and this seemed like just another one of those mornings. I usually rolled out of bed, put on my running clothes, and if I had a little extra time, I would check the morning news. This was a morning where I was a bit behind schedule, so I skipped checking the news. When I met up with my buddy, he asked, "Did you hear what happened"? He then told me that an airliner had hit the World Trade Tower. The reality took awhile to sink in. It was removed from my immediate reality, and like so much other news, it seemed like only another electronic bit of global news that I would factor in with my perceptions about what was going on in the world. We finished up our run, and I returned home and turned on the news.

Like millions of other Americans, I was stunned and shocked by what I saw. Watching the burning towers, the replays of the planes hitting the towers, the smoke, dust, and turmoil on the streets below looked like something that would only be manufactured with the advanced technological special effects and the mind of an expert movie producer. Unfortunately, the reality of this unfolding tragedy was all too real. In the weeks, months, and years that followed our world was transformed. The memories of the attack on Pearl Harbor had receded into the history books for most Americans. Those Americans old enough to remember that historical event have diminished in number as the passing years had moved on. We can also only imagine that while the news of an attack on the American Fleet at the American island in the Pacific Ocean must have been horrific and shocking enough, as defining an event as it was for world history, the environment of September 11, 2001, was quite different that that of December 7, 1941.

In 2001 Americans watched the tragic events unfold in real time. There was no definable central government that Americans could identify as the enemy. The best that could be done was to identify the Taliban government of Afghanistan as being complicit with the attackers. In 1941, the United States may have been a very strong global power, but it was not the global political, economic, and military super power that it had become sixty years later, in 2001. By 2001, there seemed to be few, if any, real challengers to American global dominion. The symbolic shock of September 11, 2001, was that a group of individuals had the audacity, and ability, to successfully carry out this horrific attack. Armed only with primitive weapons against the most advanced technological defenses ever known, they did this on American soil, in one of the most historical and greatest cities, destroying one of the most significant symbols of the American way of life. This was truly a defining event in the history of the United States and the world. History will be the judge of the effectiveness and merit of the American government's response. As Americans, however, we will be living with the immediate and future consequences of these events forever.

Many Americans have already directly experienced the deep personal loss from the death or injury of a family member, or other loved one, from the escalation and advancement of hostilities prompted by the attacks of September 11. Every war is costly in terms of the personal tragedy it creates, as well as the direct and indirect personal and social economic costs. The official administration estimate from the Congressional Budget Office is that the Iraq War will cost $500 billion over through the year 2014. This was not based upon a worst case scenario, but a mid-range scenario. A study by two researchers, Linda Bilmes, of the Kennedy School at Harvard, and Joseph Stiglitz, of Columbia University, believe these official government estimates very seriously underestimate the true costs to America. They found that the estimate provided by the Congressional Budget Office neglected to consider, or underestimated, the true economic factors of waging a war in Iraq. For example, they believe the costs of disability payments and continuing health care for the large number of returning disabled Iraq veterans has not been adequately addressed by the Congressional Budget Office cost estimate. Apart from the severe actual physical injuries, including very high levels of brain damage and loss of limbs from improvised explosive devices, these veterans are also expected to suffer from severe and extended psychological impairment from the extended services in an urban combat environment where there is no definable front line of engagement. Estimates of at least one-third of returning Iraq veterans needing extended disability, and continuing health care, are increasingly common.

Through their analysis, Bilmes and Stiglitz concluded that, using a conservative scenario, it is more likely that the costs of the war in Iraq will exceed $1 trillion. With a more moderate set of assumptions, their conclusion is that the true costs of the war in Iraq will exceed $2 trillion. Their conservative scenario assumes that U.S. troops will be withdrawn from Iraq by 2010. Their moderate assumption assumes, as does the Congressional Budget Office's estimate, that there will be a small but continuing U.S. presence in Iraq through 2015. In their more complete analysis, Bilmes and Stiglitz, recognize that there are the direct costs of war, as well as the indirect economic costs.

The direct cost would be expenses that required an actual outlay of money, such as spending on operations, Veteran Administration costs, interest on debt for war funding, as well as costs of treating the brain injuries of veterans. Indirect costs are less obvious but economically real nonetheless. These would be costs such as increases in the price of oil due to the political destabilization in an oil rich part of the world, as well as increased demand from military operations drawing limited supplies from private productive uses. It also means rising interest costs for borrowing due to the huge government demand for money to finance the war. The need of the government for funding competes with the needs of private sector individuals and businesses for the available money, meaning that it costs more for businesses to invest and stay competitive. It also means that it costs more for individuals to fund growth in the economy through continued consumption, as well as the possibility of increased insolvency among individuals and businesses as rising interest costs make it more difficult to continuing paying the variable rate debt already held by these businesses and individuals.

Bilmes and Stiglitz estimate that a truer picture of the direct costs of the war in Iraq would be over $1.2 trillion in direct costs. They estimate an additional $1 trillion for the indirect costs. These estimates of the costs of the war in Iraq do not includes operations in Afghanistan, which have been $82 trillion through the end of 2005, with $1 billion per month in continuing costs. It also does not include other costs of the War on Terror. In short, the United States is engaged in a very expensive endeavor from which it is not likely to be able to disengage any time soon. If anything, a destabilizing geopolitical environment throughout the world, as illustrated in Iran, North Korea, Venezuela, and Nigeria suggest that both the direct, as well as indirect costs, of military engagement are likely to increase rather than decrease.

The wars in Iraq and Afghanistan have been presented as one front of the War on Terrorism. The enemy facing the United States is not readily visible, except when it chooses to be. One might view the hostility as a central government military engagement against an adversary using the guerilla tactics of striking and disappearing, because it knows a direct engagement of firepower with a stronger opponent would result in certain defeat. The tactical advantage of using guerilla methodology is to strike and harm the enemy while avoiding direct confrontation. The success of this strategy results from forcing the stronger adversary to use its resources to prevent future attacks or to retaliate against the guerilla adversary.

A smart and worthy adversary will direct its attacks against high value targets that have a high probability of elimination. During the Vietnam War, the United States tried to wage a war against a guerilla army that would fade back into the jungle or general population. The attempts at eliminating this guerilla adversary by napalming and burning them to the ground were not successful. The collateral damage caused by attempts at rooting out the adversary from the general population resulted in the loss of the goodwill of the general population. The only real possibility of being successful against an adversary seeking refuge among the general population is to win the "hearts and minds" of the people. The War on Terror can be viewed as a guerilla war on a global scale against the United States and affiliated powers by radical Islamic groups and those groups with an affinity for their agenda.

The opportunities to exploit the weaknesses of the United States have not escaped its enemies. In late 2005, Al-Qaida's No. 2, Ayman al-Zawahri, issued a directive to their followers to focus their attacks against oil facilities. By the end of February 2006, an attack was made against the huge Saudi Arabian oil facility Abqaiq, the world's largest and most important crude oil processing plant handling two thirds of Saudi Arabia's oil production output. News of this event caused the price of oil to jump to over $2 a barrel. The same day this occurred, oil had earlier jumped by over $1 per barrel because of rebel attacks directed against oil interests in another important oil exporting country, Nigeria.

This is likely to be a war of attrition forcing the United States to utilize many of its declining economic, political, and military resources against a very smart enemy, whose ranks appear to be growing in number. The only real hope for the United States, and its apparently few allies, in being successful in its War on Terror, was to win the "hearts and minds" of those giving refuge to the enemies of the United States. It appears, however, that the opposite result is occurring with growing polarization between the Islamic world and the United States. Among the general population of the United States, perceptions are shifting. A *Washington Post-ABC News* poll in early 2006 found that a growing proportion of Americans express unfavorable views on Islam. A majority of Americans believe that Muslims are disproportionately prone to violence and they do not look favorably upon the United States. We have a growing polarization of cultures. In my experience, and study, I have not seen growing polarization of positions as being a favorable climate to conflict resolution. In fact, it is a good indication of a growing conflict.

Despite the direct costs of hundreds of billions of dollars the wars in Iraq and Afghanistan are projected to cost, spending on domestic security has appeared to lag behind what is necessary to protect America's home front. According to Richard Clarke, a former highly placed intelligence official in the U.S. government, "Although the United States made legal entry into the country more difficult after 9/11, it is still possible for potential terrorists to come here. Many of the new jihadis are citizens of European nations to which we grant visa-free entry. A jihadi might also come illegally, as millions of people do each year. Thus many security experts believe it is only a matter of time until another attack occurs in the United States." In the 2000, 489 million people, 127 million cars, 11.6 million maritime containers, 11.5 million trucks, 2.2 million railroad cars, 820,000 planes, and 211,000 boats passed through U.S. border inspection systems by air, land, and sea. If we take into consideration the most certainly large number of undocumented people and goods that find entry into the United States each year, can we really believe that the continental United States will not become subject to more serious terrorist attacks in the future?

One of the consequences of additional terrorist attacks in the continental United States will be reviews of what did not work with the present system, congressional hearing hearings and studies, and political fingers pointing to direct the blame towards any susceptible source. The net result, however, will commit a great deal of additional money towards creating greater domestic security with money that the United States does not have. This means the United States will have to borrow it and raise taxes. We have already seen that the United States is already so deeply in debt that it needs to borrow $60 billion per month from foreign sources. Some of the foreign sources most able to lend these funds are China and the OPEC countries accumulating vast sums of petrodollars. We must remember that the willingness to continue loaning money to finance the United States government and economy is more a marriage of economic and political convenience in contrast to an ideological love.

This marriage wears thinner the deeper into debt the United States goes, and the more polarization that occurs between the agendas of the United States and its potential foreign lenders. In January of 2006, the United States came within days of technically defaulting on its debt obligations for the first time in history. This was narrowly avoided when the Senate narrowly passed an increase in the U.S. debt limit to nearly $9 trillion, by a 52-48 vote. The worsening debt picture of the U.S. government contributes to the concern of its foreign lenders. In December, 2005, and January, 2006, foreign lenders pulled back on their willingness to continue providing cash infusions to the United States. In what is likely to be a sign of things to come, capital outflows from the United States were greater than capital inflows. U.S. Treasury debt, which is the way the government raises money to continue operating, was less in demand for investors with money to lend.

China and the United States are on a course of increasing rivalry from a trade perspective. Additionally, China has a vast need for many of the strategic resources needed by the United States. The United States is embroiled in costly wars in Iraq, Afghanistan, and in deteriorating diplomatic relationships with North Korea, Venezuela, and Iran. In general, any favorable public image is declining in most of the world. Yet, China is doing the opposite trying to win friends and influence people throughout much of the world. China's and India's rapid economic growth means they must find the raw material resources to continue fueling this growth. Their demand is pushing up the prices.

Copper is a metal that is vital to the world economy and is used in manufacturing money, plumbing, wiring, and electronics. During the 1990's, Chile's vast copper resources provided an abundant supply of this metal, which lowered the price of copper to under $.70 per pound. They supplied more than one-third of the world's copper needs. With the price low and availability of copper great, there was little economic incentive to find and develop other sources of supply. However, demand for copper from China, and other places, has greatly increased. At the same time, extensive mining of existing known reserves has depleted Chile's resources, and its production of copper slipped by 2% in 2005, which pushed the price of copper over $2 per pound. Steven Whisler, chief executive of Phelps Dodge, a large mining company, said the mining industry is "living off the fruits and labors of prospectors of 100 years ago". Mining analysts believe that because of the lack of new large scale mining projects the price of copper will remain high for at least several years. The increased demand from China has raised the price of other commodities as well over the last several years before the rapid emergence of India as another resource-hungry economy sitting at the world table. With India as a growing economic power with significant monetary resources, the global demand for energy and mineral resources will continue to push up the prices on available supplies.

Other potential large deposits of these critical resources are located in geographical areas that are remote and/or have unstable governments, such as central Africa and Mongolia. The risks and costs of developing these sites are high. For example, a huge copper deposit has been discovered in the remote Gobi region of Mongolia and is being developed by Ivanhoe Mines. Ivanhoe expects to begin production in 2008 and could become one of the largest copper mining operations in the world. The proximity of Mongolia to China, as well as China's increasing support for countries in Africa, puts China in a very favorable position to access these resources.

Another major undeveloped site is controlled by Phelps Dodge. It is the very large copper deposit of Tenke Fungurume in the Democratic Republic of Congo. This is a country which is subject to significant political instability. Consequently, a mining company is taking significant risk that its investment in developing a mine might be lost because of this political instability. The Congo has been described by Jan Egeland of the United Nations as "the world's worst humanitarian crisis". A five year war, that killed four million, left tens of thousands of armed militiamen who live by the gun. They kill and maim at will. A description, given by Harper's journalist Bryan Mealer, says "They carry out regular massacres and are known for rounding up a village's women and gang-raping them, while family members are forced to watch. Farther north, near the Ugandan border, other militias simply exterminate everything alive, and then loot and burn what's left. Often these militias butcher the dead on the battle floor and feast on the hearts and livers, both as ceremony and as a tactic of cold intimidation. Its effectiveness is superb." The idea is inescapable from this description that the challenges and costs of trying to do business in this type of environment will be very high. These types of areas contain many of the known deposits of needed and scarce resources. The copper needed to produce the circuitry for a large, flat screen TV, a new microwave oven, or the electric wiring for housing is becoming more dependent on extraction from these countries. With the increasing ability of three billion Asian consumers to purchase these types of goods, we can only expect higher future prices as material costs increase.

Countries that offer these raw material resources become strategically important trade and political powers. In the quest to win friends and influence, creating favorable relationships with these countries is a strategically strong position in which to be. Africa is a continent with an abundance of natural resources. Angola's crude oil, Zimbabwe's platinum, Zambia's copper, Congo-Brazzaville's timber, and South Africa's iron ore are prizes for a raw materials hungry economy such as China's. China has been sinking billions of dollars into the African continent in aid, special concessions, debt relief, scholarships, training, and consulting expertise. As opposed to the former European colonial powers and the U.S., China's recent emergence as an undeveloped economy puts it more in tune with the conditions in poor countries. They are less concerned than the U.S. with ideological conditions, human rights, and types of government. These conditions, coupled with the growing economic resources available to China, have created a great affinity between the Chinese and the various governing regimes of the African continent.

More than 600 Chinese-financed companies have been established in Africa since mid-1990. Some of these are manufacturing operations for regional African markets, whereas others are producing exports to the European Union or the U.S. Exports from these poorer African countries may be granted duty-free status. During this period, trade between African and China has almost quadrupled. China has been exporting machinery, electronic, and high-technology products to Africa. In addition, tens of thousands of Chinese have moved to Africa. Clearly, the Chinese have a vision of the strategic significance of a well developed relationship with the countries of Africa.

Latin America is a region that has abundant natural resource and agricultural resources. Over past years the United States has taken a keen interest, and played a very influential role, in the affairs of Latin America. The North

American Free Trade Agreement (NAFTA), was intended to create a larger and more effective region for trade between Canada, Mexico, and the United States. A similar agreement, negotiated since 1998, called the Free Trade Area Agreement (FTAA) is intended to include Central and South America into a NAFTA-like agreement. This agreement would more direct and formally extend U.S. economic interest into this region. However, things are not going according to the U.S. plan. Latin America has not been enthusiastic about this agreement. In addition to political ideological shifts away from the United States, Latin America has been courted by economic interests in Japan, the European Union, and China. The Latin American picture can be highlighted by Brazil, a huge country with abundant resources. Improvements in economic regulation, business, and government have lead to massive investment in the development of Brazil's economy. Within the next twenty-five years Brazil is expected to become one of the world's top five economies. The rapidly growing influence of China can be seen by the significant contribution it has been making to this Latin American growth story. During soybean harvest, Brazil's southern port of Paraguana will see 2600 trucks and 400 railcars lined up each day to deliver their cargo to ships headed for China. Between 200 and 2003, Brazil's exports to China quadrupled from $2.5 to over $10 billion. China's shopping list for Brazil also includes raw materials, such as iron ore, cotton, sugar, uranium, timber, and manganese. China is cementing this favorable trade relationship by investing in the development of Brazil's economic infrastructure of railways, ports, highways, and energy projects.

Brazil is not the only Latin American country willingly courted by the Chinese. Chile, Peru, Bolivia, and Venezuela appear to view China as a more favorable trade partner than its major alternative, the United States. If not altogether squeezed out from access to the rich resources of the Latin America region, the United States is in a much weaker negotiating position. Its political and economic policies are leading to its greater isolation and alienation from strategic business partners. The level of deterioration in the relationship between the important Latin American region and the United States was expressed by Hugo Chavez, Venezuela's President. Believing that the United States government was behind a failed attempt at a coup against him, he has become a vocal critic of the United States government and President George W. Bush, in particular. In March of 2006, he articulated his unfavorable views of President Bush by calling him a "donkey and a "drunkard". For the leader of one country to be calling the leader of another country names, in such a childish manner, reflects an appalling absence of statesmanship and diplomacy between these countries.

At the same time, China and other countries are capitalizing on the development of new and important strategic business relationships. As China becomes economically stronger, while the United States becomes economically weaker, political friction will increase between the two countries. As prices escalate and economic conditions worsen, the result of these circumstances will bring political pressure to the United States. Rising calls for policies to protect the perceived economic interests of the United States will result in the United States being driven into further isolation from the rest of the world, while at the same time being more dependent upon it. In mid 2005, China shocked the world by making an unsolicited offer for the large American oil company Unocal. When China National Offshore Oil Corporation (CNOOC), China's state controlled oil company, bid against Chevron for ownership of Unocal, it brought into sharp relief the potential clash of interests between the United States and China as well as the increasingly difficult position in which the United States is finding itself. Michael O'Hanlon, an international military specialist at the Brookings Institution think tank put it this way: "It does raise questions about how much of the country we are willing to sell to a Communist country that we may be fighting someday". Comments by Clyde V. Prestowitz, a former trade negotiator in the Reagan administration, and President of the Economic Strategy Institute in Washington expressed similar sentiment, "And it does raise the issue of whether this gives influence or some kind of potential importance to a government that may not always be friendly to U.S." In the end, CNOOC withdrew from the bidding process because of intense political opposition to its bid.

While these concerns are certainly prudent considerations in any type of strategic thinking about the global role of China, real problems exist from China's perspective. China must find a way to invest the huge hoard of U.S. dollars it is earning. It must also find reliable sources of the materials to sustain its growth. Wharton management professor Marshall Meyer predicts that the trend of China's continuing purchase of foreign goods and resources will continue. He believes that the likely targets of Chinese acquisition will be popular brands (the Chinese attempt to purchase Maytag), firms controlling natural resources, technological companies (the Chinese purchase of IBM's laptop division), and smaller industry outfits. A Chinese view of their thwarted attempt to purchase Unocal was expressed with words such as "unprecedented political opposition...regrettable and unjustified". An essay in the state-run Chinese news service, Xinhua, stated, "The explicit message the takeover battle sends to the world is that American business is defined by political needs...in the long run, the casualty will be on U.S. competitiveness if the market is to play second fiddle to protectionism with political patronage".

While China may be the gorilla on the block that commands attention, it is not the only gorilla on the block. About six months after the furor caused by China's Unocal bid, the media announced that DP World, a company from the United Arab Emirates, was going to be taking over managing operations at major port of the United States. This quickly became a political issue. As in the case of China's Unocal bid, the basis of the political opposition was strategic considerations. In this case, the issue was whether or not the security of the United States would be compromised by having points of entry to the United States controlled by foreign sources that might have links to its enemies.

Whether these concerns and protectionist perspectives are justified would be points of unending debate. What does not seem to be debatable is a rising sentiment towards protectionism. In March of 2006, Simon Gutierrez ended a trip to China with a warning to Beijing that protectionist sentiment is growing in the United States. He suggested that newly proposed U.S. laws aimed at threatening China were signs the United States is heading toward an era of protectionism. This trend has not escaped the notice of the World Trade Organization (WTO). This is an international organization founded in 1995 with 149 member countries by the end 2005. It was created to help smooth trade and commerce throughout the world. World Trade Organization agreements have been signed by the majority of the world's trading nations. In a report, the WTO warned that rising protectionist sentiment in the U.S. reduces the openness of the U.S. economy and would reduce growth.

Aside from the possibility of reducing economic growth, the reduction of openness from the emerging protectionist posture of the United States will tend to lead to isolationism. Isolation in a world of global inter-dependencies is a recipe for disaster. It leads to decreased constructive exposure and engagement with opposing world views. This leads to greater likelihood of misunderstanding the intentions of others with differing views of the world, and increases the chances of greater military, political, and economic conflict. This is the world we will be looking at for the future.

In the view of Dr. Ariel Cohen, Russia expert at the Heritage Foundation, U.S. policy makers are being misled by faulty geopolitical analysis of the risks and opportunities faced by the United States. Assuming that the faulty analysis is not a deliberate attempt to misled policy makers, one must conclude the U.S. global policy is being driven by erroneous understandings of the United States' relationship to other countries and governments of the world. This is resulting in the continuing loss of U.S. global prestige and a realignment of important strategic relationships in the global power balance. Russia is a potentially valuable strategic partner for the United States. In addition to the abundant natural resources of Russia, including oil and gas reserves, it is an influential diplomatic power. Collaboration in regional and global conflicts has an enormous impact on how favorable these conflicts might be resolved toward the alignment of United States' interests. Misconceptions in U.S. thinking were identified by Dr. Cohen as resulting in unsuccessful diplomatic forays. Cohen believes a complacent view was taken by Washington political analysts in anticipated the growth of strategic ties between Russia and China. The analysts believed that Russia would prefer stronger ties to the United States to counterbalance growing Chinese power. U.S. experts misjudged how alarmed both Chinese and Russian leaders would become about the regional destabilization of Central Asian governments, such as Georgia, Ukraine, and Kyrgystan. U.S. attempts at regime change in the region drove China and Russia closer together to confront what they perceived as a common peril. American propaganda attempts in this region failed to be respectful of the traditions and culture. As a consequence, American prestige and influence suffered further decline.

These fumbled diplomatic attempts have far reaching consequences. By early 2006, China and Russia were publicly embracing each other as important partners in economic and technological development. In March of 2006, President Hu Jintao of China, and President Vladimir Putin of Russia jointly inaugurated the Sino-Russian Industrial and Commercial Forum in Beijing to provide a formal opportunity for the two countries to discuss trade issues in detail. Of major strategic global significance was the agreement over energy. China has a dire need for adequate energy resources. Russia had become China's fifth largest energy supplier. China and Russia signed three deals on oil and gas supplies. One deal was between China National Petroleum Corp. (CNPC) and Transneft, a Russian pipeline company. Transneft and CNPC were to conduct a feasibility study on building an oil pipeline extension into China form the Siberian-Pacific Coast oil pipeline. Gazprom, Russia's gas giant, and CNPC also signed the agreement on building two pipelines to supply gas. At this same forum, Russia's President Putin encouraged further collaboration and expanded cooperation in the machinery, transportation, finance, education, and service sectors.

The other rapidly emerging economic powerhouse of this century will be India. India and the United States have enjoyed a friendly relationship for many years. With its industrious, highly intelligent, educated, and English speaking workforce,

India is establishing itself as an outsourcing destination for services that range anywhere from service center call answering, to engineering design, to direct delivery of high quality medical care to patients traveling there from other countries. I had a conversation with someone who had a recent hip replacement done. In the United States the operation cost $60,000. In India, the operation cost $6,000. The operation would be performed by highly trained U.S. surgeons, in state of the art surgical settings and recovery facilities. India has established a strong, and growing, competitive advantage, with its highly skilled, English speaking, and low cost work force.

The rapid economic growth of India has placed it on the same track of needing resources such as energy and the other natural resources to build and develop its economic infrastructure, for example its road system. Its geographical position in the world also places it in strategic proximity to China and Russia. We can expect greater cooperation and coordination between these countries in the future. China's Foreign Ministry Spokesman, Qin Gang expressed China's perspective by saying coordination among China, Russia, and India is in the interests of these three countries and benefits regional peace and stability. By 2005 China was rapidly catching up with the United States as India's largest trading partner. From 2004 through 2005, bilateral trade between China and India increased by 38%.

According to Nagesh Kumar, director general of Research and Information System for Developing Countries, a government funded think tank, expectations are that by 2007 China will pull ahead of the United States as India's largest trading partner. While not all analysts agree with this assessment, there is no disagreement concerning the growing importance of the relationship between China and India.

With Russia as a source of energy and raw materials, a natural alliance of a mutually beneficial nature is growing between these countries. While the United States is still a major, if not the major trading partner of India, the growing importance of the relationship between China, Russia, and India shifts the balance of negotiating power away from the United States. As a regional power block, the cooperative relationships between China, Russia, and India will have enormous political, military, and economic global significance.

The importance of these political and economic developments cannot be underestimated if an effective view of the future prospects of the United States is to be considered in financial planning and investment decision making. As competitive business pressure increases, the expected response of a well run business would be to try to reduce costs and expenses. The countries and region that can provide lower cost, high quality, manufacturing and services will strengthen at the expense of the more advanced and higher cost countries. The United States is the most developed economy in the world, but it has one of the highest costs of production as reflected in the circumstances of General Motors, and Ford Motor Company. These companies were once pillars of industry and symbols of the strength and greatness of the United States.

The irony of greatness is that it often contains the seed of its own destruction. General Motors was regarded as the bellwether of the United States. As goes General Motors, so goes America. If this is still the case, it is certainly not a good sign. General Motors is struggling for its survival. Over the years the evolution of its business enterprise has saddled it with operating and legacy costs which cripples its business competitiveness. In 2005, General Motors reported a $10.2 billion loss. In an attempt to reverse this picture, it is started to sell off some of its most profitable assets, and it has offered a retirement buyout to try to rid itself of the heavy ongoing costs it must carry. Whether it will succeed and survive is an open question. I, for one, would not consider it to be a prudent investment to put money into a company that is struggling for its survival. Those investors with more money to lose and a more speculative disposition may view this as an opportunity to purchase a distressed asset with discounted prices. In the absence of a radical makeover that will significantly change what this company is about, the likelihood of its survival does not seem high to me. Time will tell whether they can rise to the challenge of global competitors, such as Toyota, unburdened by the errors of its past ways.

Unfortunately, it does appear that the predicament of General Motors is reflective of the broader competitive conditions of many U.S. companies, as well as the United States government itself. The chapters of this book have highlighted and discussed some of the serious challenges business, governments, and municipalities face. Given these circumstances, a wise investor would do well to survey the global economic climate and identify those regions and business sectors that offer an economic climate of vigorously emerging economies likely to be sustained, definable resources for which there is an established and growing need, and ideally, favorable relationships with others in the web of global economic and political independencies. On all counts this appears to exclude investing in the United States.

What would be included in this framework would be the regional countries of Asia, Latin America, companies which own or control raw material and energy resources, as well as companies which have developed, are developing, or control the technologies to make better use of raw material and energy resources. As a hedge on deteriorating global monetary conditions, with the United States leading the way in the deterioration, investments in gold and silver will likely prove to be not only a safe harbor as a store of value, but also a growth investment as demand for these metals increases in the face of limited supply. While no one has a crystal ball, with well chosen investments in these areas, is difficult to see how these investments would not do quite well over the next ten to fifteen years.

It is important to remember, however, that all investments have risk. The key question for a wise investor is allocating to investments which have the most potential for gain relative to the risk. Additionally, for a prudent investment planning strategy, the amount of risk should be balanced with the amount of potential loss that can be tolerated financially, psychologically, and emotionally. The percentage of investment dollars allocated to these promising investments is one way to control the potential risk. A smaller percentage of this money still gives exposure to growth opportunities while reducing the amount at risk.

From a financial planning perspective, an investor should have in mind the overall investment return needed in order to reach clear financial objectives. If, for example, a 7% average annual investment return is needed in order to reach a retirement income objective, the entire portfolio should be constructed to target this return with as minimal a risk as possible. Having some percentage of a core investment position that was relatively safe would likely offer a lower investment return. Supplementation of this conservative core position with a smaller percentage of more promising growth investments may give the targeted needed average annual investment return while keeping the larger core investment positions relatively safe.

A more speculative investor, or an investor with a higher loss tolerance, could invest a higher percentage in these more promising growth areas. A common problem with speculators seems to be overconfidence in their expected outcome arising from a failure to recognize the real possible outcome of risk resulting in loss. This is a mistake for most investors who should be most attentive to defining realistic financial objectives with a reasonable expectation of successfully achieving them.

References

1. Bilmes, Linda, and Stiglitz, Joseph E., The Economic Costs of the Iraq War: An Appraisal Three Years After The Beginning of the Conflict, Paper prepared for presentation at the ASSA meeting, Boston, January 2006.

2. Economic Consequences of Terrorism, OECD Economic Outlook 71, 2002, pp. 117-140.

3. Clarke, Richard A., Battlefields, The New York Times, July 17, 2005.

4. Deane, Claudia, and Fears, Darryl, Negative Perceptions of Islam Increasing, The Washington Post, March 9, 2006.

5. Michael, Maggie, Al-Qaida No. 2 Urges Attacks on Oil Plants, Associated Press, December 7, 2005.

6. Oil Jumps $2 on Saudi Oil Blast, Reuters, February 24, 2006.

7. Flynn, Stephen E., and Bryan, Anthony, Terrorism, Porous. Borders, and Homeland Security: The Case for U.S.-Caribbean Cooperation, Council On Foreign Relations, http://www.cfr.org/publication/4844/terrorism_poroU.S._borders_and_homeland_security.html, October 21, 2001.

8. Krugman, Paul, The Chinese Challenge, The New York Times, June 27th, 2005.

9. Hulse, Carl, Senate Votes to Raise U.S. Debt Limit, The New York Times, March 16, 2006.

10. Hughes, Jennifer, U.S. Inflows Fail to Cover Trade Deficit, Financial Times, March 15, 2006.

11. Friend or Forager? How China Is Winning the

Resources and Loyalties of Africa, Financial Times, February 23, 2006.

12. Barta, Patrick, A Red-Hot Desire for Copper, The Wall Street Journal, March 16, 2006.

13. Prestowitz, Clyde, Three Billion New Capitalists; the Great Shift of Wealth and Power to the East, Basic Books, 2005.

14. Mealer, Bryan, Congo's Daily Blood; Ruminations from a failed state, Harper's Magazine, April 2006.

15. Chavez Blasts Bush as "Donkey" and "Drunkard", Reuters, March 19, 2006.

16. Wayne, Leslie, and Barboza, David, Unocal Deal: A Lot More Than Money Is at Issue, The New York Times, June 6, 2005.

17. Krugman, Paul, The Chinese Puzzle, The New York Times, June 27, 2005.

18. IBM, Maytag, Unocal...Who's Next in China's Sights, Strategic Management at Wharton, http://knowledge.wharton.upenn.edu/index.cfm?fa=viewfeature&id=1262.

19. O'Neil, John, Dubai Company Plans to Sell All U.S. Operations, The New York Times, March 15, 2006.

20. Bhadrakumar, M.K., Central Asia, Russia Regains Lost Ground, Online Asia Times, September 15, 2005.

21. Jize, Qin, China, Russia Partners in Development, China Daily, March 23, 2006.

22. Ramirez, Luis, U.S. Official Warns China of Growing Protectionist Sentiment, Voice of America, March 29, 2006.

23. Williams, Frances, WTO Warns U.S. Over Protectionist Sentiment, FT.com, March 22, 2006.

24. China, Russia, and India's Coordination Benefits

Regional Stability, Vietnam News Agency Via Thomson Dialog NewsEdge, March 22, 2006.

25. Thakurta, Paranjoy Guha, China Could Overtake U.S.'s India Trade, Asia Times Online, March 15, 2006.

CHAPTER EIGHT
Malfeasance

On December 2, 2001, the seventh largest company in the United States declared bankruptcy. With over 25,000 worldwide employees, it had been voted the most admired company by readers of *Fortune* magazine. Many of these employees believed so strongly in the company that they staked their financial future on it by investing large amounts of their retirement plans and savings in shares of the company. The collapse of Enron was stunning. A global leader in the energy markets, it had been held out as a model company by the media and business schools. McKinsey, an international business consulting firm frequently used Enron as an example in its Quarterly publication concerning how a business can establish competitive advantage over its rivals by innovation. How could so many business and investment experts have gotten the picture so wrong as to be taken by surprise at the collapse of this behemoth company?

As it turned out, Enron was a huge fraud. As a publicly traded company, Enron was required, by law, to have periodic audits by an independent and objective third party. Audits are one way that investors and other stakeholders in a company receive some assurance that the claims management makes about a company's business performance and financial health are accurate. Without this independent verification, the risks of investing or doing business with a company are increased. The role of the auditors is the watchdog of the public's interest. A major reason the United has been viewed as an attractive place to invest is because these disclosure standards created a more level playing field by requiring the disclosure of any significant and material information which would affect the decision of any potential investor, or other stakeholder.

While in theory this sounds great, in practice the system was seriously corrupted. The role of the independent and objective auditor has been filled by Certified Public Accountants. The ethical standards of this profession are intended to assure the integrity and faithful fulfillment of the auditor and the financial reporting. One of the major and highly respected Certified Public Accounting firms in the world, Arthur Andersen, had been the auditor of Enron since the company's beginning in 1985. By the year 2000, Enron had become one of Arthur Andersen's largest clients. The fees earned by Andersen in 2000 were $25 million for performing the auditing work, and another $26 million for consulting fees. Despite the fact that a financial journalist, Bethany McLean, writing an article for the March 5, 2001, edition of *Fortune* magazine, was able to identify the questionable profit making activities, and lack of transparency in Enron's reporting and handling of media questions, as Arthur Andersen was giving Enron a clean bill of financial health.

Arthur Andersen was not the only established authority singing the praises of Enron at the end stages of its life. Most financial analysts were also in the choir. In June of 2001, an analyst with Goldman Sachs described Enron as a "world class company" and a "clear leader in the energy industry". Credit rating agencies who were supposed to provide in depth analysis and assessment of the financial condition of companies were also slow to identify the warning signs at Enron. One might conclude that the reason the experts failed to recognize Enron's problems was that Enron did an excellent job hiding its fraudulent tracks. This would be a very overly generous conclusion. The expert view of Enron was probably best characterized by Goldman Sachs' analyst David Fleisher as acknowledging that Enron's "transparency" was "pretty low" and that Enron "had been indifferent to cash flow as it sought to build its business". Despite this, he rated Enron as one of the best opportunities available. Low transparency means it is difficult to determine exactly what is really going on in a business. Problematic cash flows coupled with low transparency should have been warning signs to any diligent analysis of the company.

As later events and investigation would prove, the professional "objective" views of Enron were anything but objective. The pervasive web of complicity in perpetuating this monumental fraud involved major financial institutions and business leaders bilking investors, the public, and employees of Enron out of billions of dollars. The indifference by the perpetuators of these frauds can be seen in the behavior of CEO Kenneth Lay, who, while claiming not to have had any knowledge of what was really going on, was busy reassuring investors while cashing in stock options to net more than $100 million. The CPA firm Arthur Andersen is now out of business. Major financial institutions have been fined, and Kenneth Lay's cohorts are on trial, though Kenneth Lay, himself, died of heart disease on July 5, 2006. This is probably small consolation for the thousands of people whose financial lives and careers were devastated by this event.

Shocking as the Enron collapse was, it was soon to be followed by the WorldCom bankruptcy filing in July of 2002, the largest in U.S. history. This also proved to be a result of a monumental accounting fraud. In this case investors lost $200 billion dollars. Over the next several years, one disclosure after another was made of corporate and institutional wrongdoing and fraud. A few of them:

- December 20, 2002—Every major U.S. investment bank was fined a total of $1.4 billion. These included

Merrill Lynch, Goldman Sachs, Morgan Stanley, Citigroup, Credit Suisse First Boston, Lehman Brothers Holdings, J.P. Morgan Chase, UBS Warburg, and U.S. Bancorp Piper Jaffray. They were found to have aided and abetted efforts to defraud investors.

- April 28, 2003—Goldman Sachs was found to have issued research reports which contained claims that were exaggerated or unwarranted, with opinions for which there was no reasonable basis. They were fined $110 million dollars.

- September 4, 2003—Goldman Sachs admits to violating anti-fraud laws. The firm misused insider information that the U.S. Treasury was going to suspend issuance of the thirty-year bond. Goldman Sachs agreed to pay $9.3 million in penalties. Over a six month period the firm was fined $119.3 million dollars for illegal and unethical conduct.

- September 3, 2004—The Attorney General for New York State had obtained evidence of "widespread illegal trading schemes, "late trading", and "market timing". This was estimated to have cost mutual fund shareholders billions of dollars per year.

- April 28, 2003—The Securities and Exchange Commission settled the suit it initiated against J.P. Morgan, and nine other brokerage firms, for research analyst conflicts of interest. As part of this settlement J.P. Morgan agreed to pay $25 million as disgorgement and an additional $25 million in penalties. The SEC said several "brokerage firms paid rivals that agreed to publish positive reports on companies whose shares...they issued to the public. This practice made it appear that a throng of believers were recommending these companies' shares. This was false. From 1999 through 2001, for example, one firm paid about $2.7 million to approximately twenty-five other investment banks for these so-called research guarantees, regulators said. Nevertheless, the same firm boasted in its annual report to shareholders that it had come through investigations of analyst conflicts of interest with its "reputation for integrity" maintained.

These episodes of corporate wrongdoing are an assault to our cultural myth of rectitude. The Merriam-Webster Online Dictionary defines malfeasance as "wrongdoing or misconduct especially by a public official". An objective look at the reality of our cultural behaviors strongly suggests that these instances of corporate wrongdoing are more a normal expression of our true cultural values, rather than an expression of abhorrent behavior. Recent examples of malfeasance at the federal government level include the influence pedaling case of congressional lobbyist Jack Abramoff, and the indictment of the U.S. House Congressional Representative from Texas, Tom DeLay, on corruption charges.

Jack Abramoff, formerly a powerful lobbyist, pleaded guilty to fraud, tax evasion, and conspiracy to bribe public officials. He was at the center of a wide-ranging public corruption investigation. This web of corruption was described by the head of the U.S. Justice Department, Alice S. Fisher, "The corruption scheme...is very extensive."

Tom DeLay was indicted in Texas, September, 2006, on charges involving violations of state election laws. This included money laundering and conspiring to funnel illegal corporate contributions to Republican statehouse candidates in 2002. In

2004, DeLay was criticized by the House ethics committee on issues involving misuse of his influence.

It would be tempting to dismiss these episodes as signs of our times. The evidence suggests, however, that a more appropriate dictum would be "the more things change, the more they stay the same". Government and corporate corruption, as well as their complicity with one another have been with us as long as there have been governments and other powerful interests, such as corporations. The 1980's gave us additional stellar examples of the huge destructive power of official and institutional ethical lapses. The Savings and Loan scandal was as noteworthy an event of the 1980's as the Enron's and WorldCom's of today's world. Some facts about the Savings and Loan scandal highlighted the magnitude of the events of those days taken from the book Inside Job about the Savings and Loan scandal:

- The Savings and Loan scandal was the largest theft in the history of the world. It is estimated to have been between a $400-$500 hundred billion dollar scam. This was far larger than the Enron debacle. To put it in context, rebuilding all of Western Europe after the Second World War plus ten years of air, land, and sea warfare during the Vietnam conflict did not cost as much. It was estimated that the government bail out will have cost the taxpayers around $1.4 trillion dollars.

- Through Federal government assistance via deregulation, restrictions were eased so much that S&L owners could lend themselves money.

- The Garn Institute of Finance, named after Senator Jake Garn, co-authored the deregulation of the industry and received $2.2 million from industry executives.

- Neil Bush, George Bush's son, never served time in jail for his part in running an S&L into the ground.
- Representative Fernard St. Germain, who was head of the House of Representatives banking, co-authored the deregulation and was voted out of office after other questionable dealings and was sent back to D.C. as an S&L lobbiest.
- Charles Keating, when asked if massive lobbying efforts had influenced the government officials, he replied, "I certainly hope so."
- The rip-off began in 1980 when the government raised the federal insurance on S&L's from $40,000 to $100,000 even though the typical savings account was only around $6000.
- Some of the seized assets were a buffalo sperm bank, a racehorse with syphilis, and a kitty litter mine.
- James Fail invested $1000 of his own money to purchase fifteen failing S&L's. The government reimbursed him $1.85 billion in federal subsidies.
- It sometimes took more than seven years to close failing S&L's by the government.
- When S&L owners who stole millions went to jail, their sentences were typically one-fifth that of the average bank robber.
- If the White House had stepped in and bailed out the S&L's in 1986 instead of delaying until after the 1988 elections, the cost might have been only $20 billion.

- With the money lost from the S&L scandals, the government could have provided prenatal care for every American child for the next 2,300 years.
- With the money lost from the S&L scandals, the government could have purchased five million average homes.
- The authors of Inside Job found criminal activity at every S&L they investigated.

It is not difficult to find numerous examples throughout history which illustrate the enduring aptitude of people for wrongdoing. Going back to the 1800's, we can find the story of Boss Tweed. Between 1865 and 1871, it is estimated that Boss Tweed and his cronies stole $75 to $200 million dollars from the city treasury. Convicted of forgery and larceny in 1873, Tweed was released in 1875. Immediately rearrested on civil charges, he was allowed daily visits to his family in the company of his jailor. On one of these trips, Tweed made his escape. On December 4, 1875, William Marcy "Boss" Tweed, the leader of New York City's Democratic political machine, escaped and fled to Europe.

Wrongdoing is not only a talent well developed in the United States, it also exists throughout the world and its cultures. Government, political, and business interests have no kind of monopoly on wrongdoing. Throughout our culture, the veneer of cultural rectitude serves as a facade to mask persistent and pervasive wrongdoing. Taking a look at some more mundane areas of our culture, we can see that at one of the starting points of creating responsible citizens is education. A report by the Josephson Institute of Ethics found that cheating, stealing, and lying by high school students had continued in an alarming, decade-long upward spiral. A survey of 12,000 high school students showed that the number of students admitting they cheated on an exam at least once in the past year jumped from 61% in 1992 to 74% in 2002. The number who stole something from a store within the past 12 months rose from 31% to 38%. The percentages who say they lied to their teachers and parents also increased substantially.

Along the same lines, an investigation by the Chronicle of Higher Education concluded that academic plagiarism among scholars is not unusual. An editor at the History News Network reports receiving so many tips alleging plagiarism, that they only investigate those involving well-known scholars. The article cites a study at the University of Alabama where two economists surveyed 1,200 of their colleagues, asking if they believed their work had been stolen. Forty percent answered yes.

In journalism, the objective is to report the news, which serves as the foundation for informed choice in a democracy. However, journalists are subject to the same wrongdoing malaise as those in other fields. As one example, Janet Cooke was a respected Washington Post reporter who received the Pulitzer Prize in 1981 for her story about an eight-year-old heroin addict named Jimmy, living in the slums of Washington D.C. The story turned out to be completely fabricated, and Cooke was fired from the Washington Post and returned her Pulitzer Prize. Despite this, she was rewarded with a $1.6 million movie deal. We could continue looking at other areas such as law, medicine, pharmaceuticals, scientific research, sports, taxes, workplace theft, and resume padding to find many additional examples of other forms of cheating. Our culture and society are permeated with lying, cheating, and stealing inherent parts of our lives. Notions such as integrity, honor, respect, and consideration seem like antiquated fairy tales.

So what's the point? This work is about reality, not fairy tales. It is not a moralistic sermon about how things should be. It is about how they are, and likely to be. The evidence of our observations suggests that the way things have been, the way they are, and the way they are likely to be in the future, is that lying, cheating, and stealing will continue to be an integral part of the fabric of our culture. This is not to say that there are not many personal relationships where love, caring, respect, and honor do not form a core part of those relationships. Nor does it say that there are not many people truly committed to service to humanity and altruistic action. However, as the saying goes, "a few bad apples spoil the barrel", and as we have seen, there are quite a bit more than a few bad apples. It is those events which happen on a larger scale that come back to impact us on a personal level. As has been made clear by examples of the recent past, the misdeeds of only a few people have the power to dramatically and negatively impact the lives on many thousands of people, our society, and our economy.

It is, therefore, important to understand the potential implications on a societal and personal level of widespread malfeasance and dubious ethical conduct. The investment and financial decisions we make are best done with recognition of the potential risks involved. A smart individual will want to be compensated for the risks they are taking in their financial or investment decision making. By its very nature, malfeasance, or ethical lapse, is a behavior which occurs beneath the surface. When it is discovered, it often comes as an explosion of new and relevant information, which negatively affects the outlook of a business or institution. The revelation of these events destabilizes the environment surrounding an investment. Instability increases the degree of uncertainty about the future prospects of an investment, and the risk associated with that investment has increased. As a consequence, future investors should require greater potential compensation to assume these risks. It is easy to understand the direct experience of being cheated or lied to. The less direct effects of the impact of large scale wrongdoing on our financial health are not as obvious and can be much more damaging.

We need to understand that the investment markets function as more than complex roulette wheels with black, white, and numbers being replaced by stock and mutual fund ticker symbols. When we invest our money, we are participating in a huge financing system. Economic progress takes place because someone has an idea or project they would like to see happen. If they can get enough other people to believe in the idea enough to invest in it, also known as providing investment capital, the project can get going. The same principle is involved whether we are talking about an individual entrepreneur or the project of a major corporation or government. The level of organization for acquiring financing becomes more complex, but the principles are the same. Economists, and financial types, refer to these concentrations of investment money as capital formation. In order for an economy to be healthy, there has to be enough investment money around to fund the development and expansion of the economic infrastructure, such as the building and maintenance of roads, laying the groundwork for future ideas through education and research, and technological and communications development. Uncertainty in the investment environment increases when investors believe their property rights are not adequately protected by the rule of law.

Malfeasance ultimately means that property, power, or other rights, are misappropriated. As investors perceive an increase in the risk to their investments because of a higher probability that acts of malfeasance will occur, they will demand higher investment returns to compensate for these risks. This increases the costs of financing newer projects or economic development. It will slow down economic development. In the unusually clear words of former Federal Reserve Board Chairman Alan Greenspan who noted on July 16, 2002,

"Well-functioning markets require accurate information to allocate capital and other resources, and market participants must have confidence that our predominately voluntary system of exchange is transparent and fair...Falsification and fraud are highly destructive to free-market capitalism and, more broadly, to the underpinnings of our society."

In a world where mega amounts of investment capital can be electronically transferred across international boundaries in seconds, a country or region must have and maintain a competitive advantage in order to continue attracting investment dollars from the global financial markets. The United States has had a reputation of having a very developed property rights system. The perception was that whatever other business risks might be involved with an investment because of information disclosure requirements for publicly traded companies and the perception of equitable treatment under the law, the risk of having investment assets misappropriated because of corporate of governmental misconduct was minimal. Whether this perception was myth or reality, there was enough concern after the discovery of the rash of corporate wrongdoing by the end of 2001, that the United States Congress enacted the Sarbannes-Oxley Act in July of 2002. The intent of this act was to restore the public confidence in the investment markets which had been severely damaged by regular and ongoing revelations of corporate misdeeds.

With all the apropos of political hullabaloo to reassure the public that something really was being done to combat corporate misdeeds, President Bush characterized this law as "the most far-reaching reform of American business practices since the time of Franklin Delano Roosevelt." The idea behind the Act was to prevent deceptive accounting and corporate management misbehavior and create greater accountability for corporate fraud by imposing greater criminal penalties and more stringent financial information disclosure requirements. Despite the public relations campaign surrounding this Act, there were many other voices claiming that the rapid passing of this Act was little more than a political product to placate an outraged public.

The Sarbannes-Oxley Act is one more way in which the costs of malfeasance significantly impact our economic environment of our country. Moreover, because of the central role of the U.S. economy in the world, anything which significantly impacts U.S. economy, will impact the global economy. Since how well or poorly investments perform is ultimately determined by economic and political events, sooner or later, when the costs of malfeasance become large enough, they will present a headwind to good investment performance. Zhang, a researcher at the William E. Simon Graduate School of Business Administration, studied the economic impact of the Sarbannes-Oxley Act. Because of the direct costs of compliance with increased government regulation including legal and accounting fees, indirect costs including diversion of productive business resources toward compliance issues, and expected future costs of anti-business legislation, Zhang estimates this translates into a $1.4 trillion loss of market value.

Despite what sometimes may seem to be a freewheeling and casino type approach to investment decision making, a smart investor understands that any inherent value in the stock of a company is derived from the current and future profitability prospects of the company. If the company's operating expenses or costs of doing business increase, the potential profitability of the company decreases. As a consequence, it would be realistic to expect that the price of the company's stock would decline or grow more slowly. The translation to your personal economic circumstances is that your investments suffer. This loss comes out of your pocket, whether it is your retirement account, personal investment account, or some other investment that fares poorly because of a decline in business competitiveness due to increased regulatory expenses.

The Sarbannes-Oxley Act is not something most people would find meaningful in the context of their normal experiences. To put it in earthly terms, the Act was presented as a way to keep the foxes out of the henhouses by increasing the monitoring requirements to assure that accurate information about the company is presented to the public. It makes officers and directors of a company more personally accountable for the accuracy of this information by punishment if they fail to do so. Many critics of the Act say that it is costly and ineffective. As might be expected, the business community is, in general, a major critic of the Act. Their concerns center on the high costs of compliance. CFO Magazine did a survey of executives, as reported in their August 2003 issue, and found that 70% of those responding did not believe that the benefits of the Act are worth the costs. Financial Executives International found that the first year cost estimate of complying with the Act is almost $3 million for 26,000 hours of internal work, 5,000 of external work, and additional audit fees of $823,000. Sixteen percent of the respondents had sales revenue below $100 million, and Fifty four percent had sales revenue above $1 billion.

The viewpoint of critics of the Act might be viewed as self-serving. Is it just the fox objecting that it is more difficult to enter the henhouse? The point may be valid, and the experts concur. Unfortunately, the evidence also suggests that there are a sufficient number of business and government leaders who cannot be trusted and that additional monitoring and significant consequences are needed to reduce the likelihood of institutionalized theft. No one likes the added expense of locks and security systems on their homes and businesses to protect themselves and their property. A fact of life in our world is that the risk to us of not having these things is unacceptable.

We pay for prevention in the hope that it will be less costly than then the cure. The reality is, however, that this cat and mouse model means a continual process where some preventive remedy is put in place by the "good guys" to prevent malfeasance from occurring. This is followed up by the "bad guys" finding some way around these preventive remedies. This requires a never-ending escalation of cost and commitment of resources. Unless some fundamental change occurs in human behavior, this is likely to be a pattern which continues. Based upon thousands of years of cross-cultural history, it would be nothing short of a miracle for any fundamental behavioral change of human behavior to occur. Consequently, it is highly probable we can expect more of the same.

Technology is a wondrous advance in the field of human endeavor. It has provided us with the ability to hugely amplify our abilities to effectively accomplish what it is we set out to do. Unfortunately, comparable advances have not occurred in the wisdom of what we set out to do. As potentially good as technology is, it has also given us the ability to take what appear to be fundamental human behaviors and transform them into potentially globally devastating actions. Wars could once be waged with sticks, stones, spears, swords, bows and arrows, then guns. While we increased our capacity in the scale of destruction possible, nothing compares with our nuclear, biological, or chemical destructive capacity. The stakes of human beings behaving like human beings have grown incredibly huge because of our technological prowess. In the past wrongdoing and malfeasance were contained in a relatively localized economic environment, and the negative effects limited. Because of the integration and interconnectedness of the many complex financial systems of our economy, the scale of negative outcomes from malfeasance has increased to the point where major institutions, governments, and economies can be destroyed.

An example in our recent economic history of how our intertwined financial system can unravel through a potential domino effect can be seen in the undoing of the prominent hedge fund Long Term Capital Management (LTCM). LTCM was started in 1994 by the former head of bond trading at Salomon Brothers, John Meriwether. Meriwether recruited such financial luminaries as Myron Scholes and Robert Carhart Merton to its board of directors. Scholes and Merton are considered among the intellectual pillars of modern financial theory. They shared the Nobel Prize in Economics in 1997. If there was ever a way to paint the veneer of rocket science over financial theory, LTCM succeeded in doing it. Their trading systems were based upon complex mathematical formulations and relationships. The impression that it gave was of a "can't lose" system. Initially, LTCM was very successful. Through the end of 1997 it had annual rates of return of around 40%. Moreover, it did this with relatively little volatility, which is a financial measure of risk. So far, so good. LTCM was the hero of Wall Street.

Because the Wall Street bankers and institutions were starry-eyed about LTCM, they made ample amounts of investment capital available to them on extremely favorable terms. This allowed LTCM to borrow against its investment equity at very favorable rates and use the proceeds to make additional investments. This is known as trading on margin and is a way to leverage an initial investment to a much higher amount invested. Doing this amplifies the potential gains on the original investment. To illustrate, let's say you have $100,000 invested. If you use the $100,000 as collateral and borrow an additional $100,000 against it, at an interest rate of 5% you now have $200,000 to invest. If you earn 10% on the $200,000, you have made $20,000. Since you borrowed $100,000 at 5%, you have $5,000 of interest cost on the borrowed money. Subtracting this from your $20,000, you have left $15,000 of profit on a $100,000 investment. Using leverage, you have amplified your potential gain to 15%, instead of 10%.

LTCM used this principle to leverage $7.3 billion of investor's money into $120 billion of investments. This represented an investment of $16 of borrowed money for every $1 of investor's money. As if this leverage were not enough, LTCM returned $2.7 billion of capital to its investors. This meant it now had $25 of borrowed money invested for each $1 of investor's money. Given our illustration about how borrowing enough to just double your investment can amplify your potential investment returns, it is easy to see why investors would be very pleased with LTCM.

A problem with using leverage to amplify the performance results in an investment portfolio is that it can also work in the opposite direction when losses occur. If we assume, from our illustration above, that instead of having a 10% gain, we had a 10% loss on $200,000, we would have lost $20,000 plus $5,000 from the 5% interest cost on the $100,000 we borrowed for investment purposes. We would have lost $25,000 on our $100,000 investment, a 25% loss. Considering the huge leverage LTCM had of $25 of borrowed money for $1 of investor capital, as opposed to the $2 to $1 ratio of our example, we can see that the potential for loss would be huge should events take a turn for the worse. The mathematical sophistication and stature of the LTCM investment strategy lead to the belief that LTCM would be immune from the risk of a potential huge loss.

According to Wikipedia, a free online encyclopedia, hubris is a word taken from the ancient Greece that "referred to a reckless disregard for the rights of another person resulting in social degradation for the victim." Our modern usage of the word refers to excessive pride, or self-confidence, which results in a bad outcome. A different expression of this idea is from Proverbs 16:18 that "pride goeth before a fall". LTCM, their lenders and investors, were to experience this all too vividly. By July of 1998, market conditions deteriorated rapidly, and LTCM experienced significant losses. The following month the Russian government devalued their currency, the ruble, causing global turmoil in the investment markets.

Within months the losses at LTCM were so large that its very survival was at risk. By September, people who knew LTCM's situation expected that it would not be able to continue without outside assistance. Because of the huge amount of money loaned to LTCM by major Wall Street firms and banks, there was growing alarm at the global financial consequences of a LTCM failure. While not everyone agrees, the fact is that concern was so great that the consequences of such as failure could cause a major calamity in global financial markets necessitating the intervention of the Federal Reserve

Bank of the United States. They facilitated additional funding for LTCM to continue long enough for a more orderly winding up of the affairs of this investment company.

The story of LTCM is more one of arrogance, pride, and over-confidence with the potential of leading to a worldwide financial catastrophe. It more represents the potential consequences of the frailty of human character than the dishonesty and deceit of acts of malfeasance. The point of the use of LTCM as an example is to illustrate how the global financial system can be a house of cards which is held together by huge concentrations of money and power. Compromising the strength of this cement through poor judgment or acts of malfeasance can cause this house of cards to come tumbling down. This was seen with the failure of Barings Bank. Barings Bank was a 200 year old bank in England. It was one of the most respected and oldest banks of England used by the Queen and members of her family. One individual, Nick Leeson, brought about the failure of this mighty institution through his misdeeds, causing it to become bankrupt.

High concentrations of money and power provide trigger points for economic calamity that can be brought about by relatively few individuals or institutions. The potential harm which can arise from acts of malfeasance represents a moral hazard in our investment environment. Some financial theorists would argue that this risk is "priced in" to our investments so that what we invest in is fairly valued with respect to its risks. I see little sound rationale to accept this point of view. Risks that can be perceived and quantified can perhaps be priced in to arrive at an estimate of fair value for an investment. Many risks, such as the moral hazard of malfeasance, cannot be effectively quantified. The media, institutional, and governmental approach to representing these types of risks to the general investor seems to be to marginalize these risks. This approach gives a false sense of security and the impression that these risks are non-significant. This may be necessary to manage the perceptions of the general investor and retain confidence in the financial markets. From the perspective of the individual, this approach breeds complacency where there should be vigilance in the wise management of one's assets.

It is necessary, therefore, to consider what the potential negative impacts could be to our personal financial planning and investment decisions were the failure of a pivotal economic institution to occur because of acts of malfeasance. One way to do this is to look a possible scenario in which a significant financial disruption occurs and examine the potential consequences. Consider the hypothetical case of Fannie Mae. Fannie Mae is an acronym for the Federal National Mortgage Association. It is a government sponsored independent corporation. It buys mortgages on the secondary market, bundles them, and resells them as mortgage backed bonds to investors. Through this process, liquidity is created for additional mortgage lending. This process supports the housing market as well as all the economic activity associated with a strong housing market. As one might imagine, Fannie Mae plays a central role in the economic health of the United States, and consequently, the world. Let's assume a financial crisis occurred with Fannie Mae that seriously impaired its solvency.

The fact of the matter is that while we are calling this a hypothetical example to illustrate potential negative outcomes, Fannie Mae was actually involved in a very significant accounting scandal. The matter was originally brought to light by a Federal Agency, the Office of Federal Housing Enterprise Oversight (OFHEO). Referring to Fannie Mae, within their report they stated, "The matters detailed in this report are serious and raise concerns regarding the validity of previously reported financial results, the adequacy of regulatory capital, the quality of management supervision, and the overall safety and soundness of the Enterprise." The scandal brought about the resignation of its CEO, Franklin Raines, and CFO Timothy Howard on December 21, 2004. Fannie Mae was also forced, by the Securities and Exchange Commission, to restate its accounting records over a three and a half year period. It had to recognize over $9 billion dollars of losses that had been hidden from the public.

While Fannie Mae seems to have emerged from this financial crisis, in our hypothetical scenario we will assume it was not able to do this. We only need look at a study undertaken over a two year period by economists and researchers at the OFHEO. The goal of the study was to examine the issue of risk and the impact of institutions like Fannie Mae in the nation's housing and financial markets. Various scenarios and outcomes were considered. In considering these scenarios they state, "Every firm—-even one that has consistently been highly profitable, is well capitalized and highly liquid—-has some probability of failure. Financial history is replete with stories of highly regarded firms that faltered, became illiquid, and failed...The future differs from the past in unexpected ways, and sometimes those differences can be great. The consequence is that unexpected events can cause institutions to suffer losses from exposures that neither they nor their regulators viewed as significant or which few observers were even aware." If there were any risk that would fit the description of these unexpected events, it would the risk of acts of malfeasance.

In a case scenario considered in this study, an enterprise such as Fannie Mae unexpectedly incurs large losses. At the same time other financial institutions are in a weakened position. Investors become concerned about the survival of this enterprise and consequently the safety of the bonds they have issued. This concern leads to widespread selling of these bonds by investors. This leads to large declines in the market prices of these bonds, in this case mortgage-backed securities. There are many ways in which this scenario can unfold from here. One outcome could be that if the sell-off of these bonds turns into a panic with many investors rushing for the door at the same time, it would likely result in an inability to easily sell these bonds, a condition known as illiquidity. Given how pervasive mortgage-backed securities are throughout the financial system, these problems could spread to other financial institutions such as insurance companies, banks, thrifts, pension, mutual funds, and any other financial institutions that have high concentrations of these bonds in their portfolios. The result is a very negative impact on the financial sector, and the U.S. and global economies. As the report goes on to say, "If the government does not prevent a financial crisis, the potential decline in aggregate economic activity may be very large."

Given the challenges already facing the government in adequately funding existing operations, we would have to question the ability of the government to effectively respond to a monumental financial crisis. We have had the opportunity to witness the governmental response to devastating crises in recent years. To say the effectiveness of response has been uneven would be a generous statement to the thousands of people displace by hurricane Katrina or the hundreds of thousands of Americans having difficulty coping with rising energy and medical costs. Even were the government to intervene in a monumental financial crisis, the creation of the needed liquidity may well result in hyper-inflation. If they did not intervene, we would be looking at a collapse of the global economic system. It surely seems as if it would be another case of damned if you do, damned if you don't.

No one can adequately determine the probability of such a devastating financial event. Those who venture to offer a low probability to such an event might well consider the low probability events of Hurricane Katrina, or the Asian Tsunami of recent years. It only takes the occurrence of one low probability event to end life as we know it. If we acknowledge the possibility of such a hugely negative financial event, the question we need to consider in our financial planning and investment choices is what our proactive response should be. As a defensive investment consideration, our first rule should be to protect the value of what we already lucky enough to have. We would like to increase the value of our investments, and we most definitely don't want to lose value. What investments would be likely to lose value, and what investments would be most likely to retain value in such circumstances as we have been considering.

As identified in the scenario analysis, bonds and financial institutions would appear to be the ones to take the initial brunt of a collapsing financial system. To the extent that one could timely exit these types of investments at a time of financial crisis, it is questionable as to what one's proceeds might be worth. While these types of investments have traditionally been viewed as conservative investments, this perspective was based upon a time when there was more prudent and conservative financial management exercised in our financial system than there is today. In today's world, it should no longer be assumed that what was true yesterday is true today. The corrosive effects of malfeasance and imprudent financial management have eroded the core of the global financial system. The very real possibility of continued deterioration in the pillars of the global financial system cannot be ignored in order to make wise financial planning and investment decisions.

When considering which assets and investments might best retain and even increase in value, we can go back to the basic economics of supply and demand. Assets which are tangible, and which satisfy a basic need, are likely to retain and increase their value. Investments which represent a direct claim to these types of assets are likely to follow suit. Precious metals, strategic assets such as energy, and natural resources will retain a residual value in the event of a collapse of the financial system. In fact, because a collapse in the financial system is likely to cause an exodus to assets and investments such as these, it is quite likely that an increase in the value of these would occur, perhaps dramatically so. Investors who have acted proactively in taking positions in these investments are likely to do quite well during the panicked turmoil of a major financial crisis.

It should be noted that a wisely constructed investment portfolio should attempt to manage different future possibilities in accordance with the risk tolerance of the investor. While it is my belief of the very real possibility of a disastrous financial calamity, it would not be wise to plan on this as a foregone conclusion. Consequently, financial choices and investment decisions should try to strike a balance between better and worse case scenarios. The balance can and should shift as fundamental political and economic events necessitate it. This is a thinking person's process, however. It requires the thoughtful consideration and response to ongoing events in the world, but not a knee-jerk reaction to them. While it may be easier and comforting to believe that a mechanical investment management process will result in your financial security, it is more likely that you are buying a bill of goods which will more accommodate an institutional agenda than successfully meeting your financial planning goals. There is no place left in today's world for complacency and old unchallenged assumptions in investment and financial perspective.

References

1. Corporate Ethics, Creative Investment Research, Inc., http://www.creativeinvest.com.

2. SEC, NY Attorney General, NASD, NASAA, NYSE

3. and State Regulators Announce Historic Agreement to Reform Investment Practices, Securities and Exchange Commission, http://www.sec.gov/news/press/2002-179.htm.

4. SEC Sues GOLDMAN SACHS For Research Analyst Conflicts of Interest Firm To Settle With SEC, NASD, NYSE, NY Attorney General, and State Regulators, Securities and Exchange Commission Release No. 18113, April 28, 2003.

5. State Investigation Reveals Mutual Fund Fraud, Office of the New York State Attorney General Eliot Spitzer, September 3, 2003.

6. Hamilton, Stewart, The Enron Collapse, IMD International, IMD-1-0195, May 3, 2003.

7. WorldCom Malfeasance Revealed, CBS News, June 10, 2003, http://www.cbsnews.com/stories/2003/07/07/national/main562014.shtml.

8. WorldCom, The Cheating Culture, http://www.cheatingculture.com/worldcom.htm.

9. Hulse, Carl, and Blumenthal, Ralph, DeLay Decides to End Career in Congress, New York Times, April 4, 2006.

10. Schmidt, Susan, and Grimaldi, James V., Abramoff Pleads Guilty to 3 Counts, Washington Post, January 4, 2006.

11. Pizzo, Stephen, Fricker, Mary and Paul Muolo, *Inside*

Job: The Looting of America's Savings and Loans, New York: McGraw-Hill Publishing Co., 1989.

12. Boss Tweed Escapes, Today in History: December 4, http://memory.loc.gov/ammem/today/dec04.html.

13. Survey Documents Decade of Moral Deterioration: Kids Today Are More Likely To Cheat, Steal, And Lie Than Kids 10 Years Ago, Josephson Institute of Ethics, 2002 Report Card, http://www.josephsoninstitute. org/Survey2002/survey2002-pressrelease.htm.

14. Bartlett, Thomas, and Smallwood, Scott, Four Academic Plagiarists You've Never Heard Of: How Many More Out There? Chronicle of Higher Education, A Special Report, December 17, 2004.

15. Zhang, Ivy Xiying, Economic Consequences of the Sarbannes-Oxley Act of 2002, William E. Simon Graduate School of Business Administration, February 2005.

16. Hilzenrath, D.S., Weisman, J. and Vandehei, J., How Congress Rode a "Storm" to Corporate Reform, The Washington Post, July 28, 2002.

17. Dowd, Kevin, Too Big to Fail? Long-Term Capital Management and the Federal Reserve, Cato Institute Briefing Papers No. 52, September 23, 1999.

18. Rawnsley, Judith H. and Leeson, Nick, Total Risk: Nick Leeson and the Fall of Barings Bank, HaperBusiness, 1995.

19. Report of Findings to Date, Special Examination of Fannie Mae, Office of Compliance, Office of Federal Housing Enterprise Oversight, September 1, 2004.

20. Systemic Risk: Fannie Mae, Freddie Mac and the Role of OFHEO, Office of Federal Housin Enterprise Oversight, February 2003.

CHAPTER NINE
Part One
Investments

Throughout this book we have looked at the mega-trends which will affect your personal financial circumstances. These mega-trends are like a number of economic and political Hurricane Katrina's from which we get an occasional high wind gust. As of yet, we have not felt the full brunt of their impact, and there is the very real possibility that several of these may hit our economic landscape simultaneously. It is not likely that we can change their course. Our best course of action is to try to prepare for them, as best as we are able, by finding safe harbors for our assets and preparing for the opportunities that may also present themselves to us.

Our observations and analyses lead to several promising investment areas, as well as offer guidance as to our personal financial decision-making. These areas repeatedly come up as potentially attractive in the likely event that one or more of these mega-trends will lead to a global financial debacle. As such, it presents us with an overarching theme that can and, in my opinion, should act as a structural foundation for a mid to long term investment strategy. I consider three-seven years as the time-frame for a mid-term investment strategy, with seven years and beyond as a long-term investment strategy.

At this juncture, it is important to distinguish between a trading, or speculative strategy, and an investment strategy. Many people have lost sight, or never even had in sight, this distinction. The temptation to try to make a fast buck is what drives the speculative trading strategy. For most people this temptation becomes too overpowering to resist when they perceive what appears to be everyone around them making these fast bucks. In recent years we can think of the dot.com boom, which spawned a bevy of day traders who believed that all they had to do to become wealthy was trade stocks throughout the day, perhaps with the assistance of a sophisticated, can't lose software program alerting them to the ideal times to buy and sell. Alternatively, if they did not day trade, they may have listened to the advice of stockbrokers, or other financial service salespeople knowing little more than they did. The unfortunate result was the same when this bubble burst in the year 2000. Many people lost a great deal of money. It was extremely sad to speak with new clients who had come to my office. They would show me their account statements which, in some cases, had lost 50%-60% of their value. The blow to their financial position might have been easier to take had the losses only been from some of the incredible investment returns that were generated during the 1990's. Unfortunately, as is always the case, some were late-comers to the party who had put their money into these markets not too long before they crashed. I will always remember, for example, the woman who had come to me for advice after having lost 60% of a modest inheritance her father had left her. Like so many others who had come to me in the aftermath, it seemed as if she half-expected that I could use a magic wand and make her money reappear. I wish I had this power, but alas, I do not. A lesson here is that risk is a very real thing. It is more than an intellectual abstraction. It actually does mean that you can lose money; sometimes quite a lot of it, very quickly. Working with people to plan their financial futures, it is tragic when someone takes what could have been a strong baseline of future financial security and losses it through mismanagement or otherwise poor financial decision-making.

Unfortunately, people find some lessons more difficult to learn than others. With the passing of this speculative frenzy, the real estate market became the next beneficiary of the speculators affections. This gave rise to such practices as "flipping" properties. Investors would buy properties, sometimes that had not even finished being constructed, and turn around and sell them. As with the dot.com boom, this is an example of the "greater fool" theory of investing. In this theory it doesn't really matter what you pay for something, as long as you can find a greater fool to pay you more for it. When the music stops is when the problems begin. This frenzy was encouraged by the very low interest rate, and easy credit policy, of the Federal Reserve Bank of the United States, and embraced by our political leaders for the stimulating effects on the economy. All parties end at some point, however. As of the middle of 2006, increasing evidence is surfacing which suggests that this party is also now ending. The likely result will be another massive loss of money for a great many people.

While there may be nothing inherently wrong with speculation, it is not appropriate for the many people who cannot afford to lose whatever moderate financial resources they have managed to acquire. These resources are to assist in providing at least a baseline of financial security throughout their lives. A general rule is that one should put at risk more than one can afford to lose. The problem, however, is that risk has many faces. As an example, one can invest in a lower yielding investment such as a United States Treasury Bill. One can be relatively assured of having one's principal invest and a small amount of interest returned at a specified point in the future. The problem over the longer term, however, is that if inflation is high, the interest earned may not even be sufficient to keep up with inflation. If we consider taxes also reducing the amount of interest really earned, one may be getting their principal investment returned, but losing the purchasing power their original investment had. Here we are trading off one type of risk, the risk of having our principal investment returned, against another type of risk, which is the risk that our purchasing power will not be returned. The consequence is that one way or another, we must assume some type of risk, willingly or unwillingly. We balance the risks and rewards among the many investment opportunities and financial choices we must make. This is what a prudent, and well thought-out, investment strategy is about.

There is an alternative to the speculative approach, and it requires the prudent assessment of the potential risks and rewards of the investment environment, as well as what the monetary requirements are for us to meet our financial needs and objectives. If our financial needs and objectives are out of whack with what is financially realistic, there will be an inclination to accept the invitation for reckless speculation. In building a mid to longer term investment portfolio we want investments which will be durable, based upon sound economic principles, and reflect the political and global realities, which do, and will continue to, shape the economic environment. The areas we have focused on in this book define several investment themes which should serve as the core foundation for a prudent investment strategy designed to provide at least a baseline of financial security for ourselves and our families. While not without risk, these themes provide the conceptual framework within which we can think about the merits, or lack thereof, of investment choices, and other financial decision making.

Our analysis has given us both the broader areas of investment to avoid, as well as those which may provide exceptional opportunity. The construction of an investment portfolio is not quite as simple as merely putting your money into a potentially profitable investment. While broad direction may be given as to where to invest, what specifically to invest in is another question.

Let's start our foray into developing a longer term investment strategy by considering energy. In our chapter on the Energy Situation, we have seen how an imbalance the between supply and demand for oil, the primary energy source for modern civilization, is out of balance. The demand for oil continues to grow, while at the same time the sources of oil are becoming more and more constrained. The evidence shows that the existing proven reserves are decreasing. Moreover, even these existing reserves are proving more and more difficult to access, at least for the United States. The competition from other growing economies, such as China and India, is also rapidly growing. Their increasing economic muscle is making them more and more formidable rivals. The world needs energy, and a growing amount of it, to continue to function. The question is not whether we will run out of oil tomorrow. Some of the relevant questions are: what will the price of oil be in the near and distant future, how rapidly the price will increase, what are the implications of increasing oil prices, what will the alternatives be, and how rapidly will they be developed? From an investment perspective, however, it is difficult to see how making well selected investments in the energy sector would not prove to be lucrative over a mid and longer term investment horizon. A fundamental, and intuitively true, law of economics is the law of supply and demand. In accordance with this law, as the demand for something grows and the supply is limited, or even decreasing, we can expect the price of it to increase. It follows that if one wishes to make money, one should own what will be in increasing demand and limited supply. In this case we are discussing oil in particular and energy, in general. If we lose sight of the bigger picture of the global energy situation, as highlighted in our chapter on Energy, it is easy to become confused and mislead by the market noise of shorter term events. As examples, let's consider some of the events purporting to impact the price of oil, at least on a daily basis. Performing a Google News search with the term "oil price" from August 23, 2006 to August 25, 2006, yields 1,900 news items. Within this short period of time, some of the headlines stating what is responsible for the price of energy are:

> *Crude Oil Rises as Storm Forms, Eni Workers Abducted in Nigeria*
> Bloomberg—August 25, 2006
> *Ongoing Tightness In Oil Market Supporting Prices*
> FN Arena News—August 25, 2006
> *Regulators Seek To Curb Energy Funds*
> Long Island Business News—August 25, 2006
> *Oil Prices Up on New BP Cut*
> The Australian—August 24, 2006
> *Traders Return, Push Up Oil Prices*
> August 24, 2006
> *Iranian Nuclear Issue Causes Prices to Fluctuate*
> People's Daily Online, China—August 24, 2006
> *Oil Prices Slip As Gas Supplies Rise*
> CBS News, New York—August 23, 2006
> *Oil Prices Hold Steady At $72 a Barrel*
> CBS News, New York—August 22, 2006
> *OIL FUTURES: Brent Down On Pft Taking*
> Cattlenetwrok.com—August 23, 2006

This small sampling of the daily events affecting the price of oil within a three day period shows that the price of oil was down, holding steady, and increasing. Some of the reasons given for these price changes were political turmoil, forces of nature, oil trader manipulation, supply disruptions, and supply in excess of what was expected. One could select, at random and at any time, another time-frame and the result would be very much the same. While this type of information may be of value to a speculative trader, for a mid to longer term investor, it does not amount to much more than market noise. The fact of the matter is that few of these events have significant implications affecting the energy picture described in our chapter on Energy. An exception would be that a deteriorating situation, in a structural component having longer term implications, such as with Iran, would be something that should get ones attention. An event like this would likely accelerate the increase in the price of oil. The ripple effects of an event like this would travel far and wide to other areas of our investment environment. None of the events cited, however, suggests there is anything that would ease the longer term energy supply shortage.

This means that well selected investments in the energy sector would likely experience the price volatility of the underlying events affecting the near term price of oil. This may, at times, occur for extended periods of time. Unless, however, there is some global structural change in supply and demand, the underlying longer term value, and potential investment return, of these investments would be intact.

Energy

The implications for us in constructing a mid to longer term investment portfolio is that what we would like to have in our portfolio are strong core investment positions. A characteristic of these positions would be investments which will, at the very least, retain an inherent value and have a high probability of increasing value of future years. This profile is consistent with the characteristics investment in the energy sector offered to us.

If we conclude that investing in energy is a core position in our portfolio, the next question that must be addressed is what form of energy investments, and how to do so. There are stocks, mutual funds, exchange traded funds, limited partnerships, private deals, and, I am sure many more configurations you may be solicited with in some way. There are different forms of energy such as oil, gas, nuclear, solar, hydrogen fuel cells, biofuels, wind, and an increasing number of new technologies promising alternative fuels sources. Unless, however, you are prepared, and have the desire, to develop some business and investment expertise in the analysis of these different ventures, investing in a diversified spectrum of these opportunities would be the most prudent course to take, at least substantial core positions in your investment portfolio. These investments would take the form of mutual funds, or exchange traded funds with exposure to the energy sector. I tend to be partial toward the exchange traded funds (ETF) because of, among other reasons, they have lower internal operating costs than mutual funds, they tend to be more tax-friendly to the investor, they can be bought and sold throughout the day, as opposed to mutual funds, in which the investor must wait until the end of the day to buy, or sell the fund.

Having said this, however, there are times when a low internal operating cost, no-load mutual fund may be a more cost effective way to invest. For example, if you are investing smaller amounts on a regular basis, the transaction cost, small though it may be, can be avoided by investing in a no-load mutual fund. You will need to give some thought to the trade-off between the amount you save on your transaction costs and the advantages of using an ETF. If for example, you are investing $50 a month, even a small $10 transaction fee to purchase an ETF represents a substantial percentage of your initial investment that has to be overcome by an equally substantial investment return just to break even. Additionally, there may be circumstances, such as with a 401(k) investment, where ETF's are just not an available option. In fact, you may not even have a clearly definable choice for investing in a pure energy fund. In this case, the best you can do is to examine your investment choices and find the mutual funds within them which have a high percentage of energy investments within the fund.

You should also keep in mind that at some point investing in energy will likely become a mania, such as investing in dotcoms, or most recently, real estate. When this happens all sorts of promoters come out of the woodwork, with all sorts of schemes, promising all sorts of things. I have already seen some evidence of this beginning to occur. Retaining a balanced perspective and a prudent approach will be your best allies in this event. Once you have thoughtfully established your strategy, you should only change it through careful consideration of the consequences. Being convinced, for example, that you are being offered a ground floor, no lose deal, with very high investments returns, in a short period of time would not exactly constitute a well thought through consideration.

Examples of potential investments in the energy might include:

Exchange Traded Funds trade like a stock. They have trading flexibility. They can be bought or sold intraday on the exchanges.

They are like index funds in that they are constructed to track benchmark indexes, have low expense ratios, and low turnover. This offers the benefits of low cost, tax efficiency, transparency, risk management, liquidity, modularity and cleaner strategy implementation.

The following are examples of some of the Exchange

Traded Funds available in the energy sector. Note that there are hundreds of ETF's, with the number growing rapidly because of their growing popularity.

Dow Jones U.S. Energy Sector Index Fund (IYE)

The Dow Jones U.S. Energy Sector Index Fund seeks investment results that correspond generally to the price and yield performance, before fees and expenses, of U.S. energy stocks, as represented by the Dow Jones U.S. Oil & Gas Index.

Dow Jones U.S. Oil & Gas Exploration & Production Index Fund (IEO)

The Dow Jones U.S. Oil & Gas Exploration & Production Index Fund seeks investment results that correspond generally to the price and yield performance, before fees and expenses, of the Dow Jones U.S. Select Oil Exploration & Production Index.

Dow Jones U.S. Oil Equipment & Services Index Fund (IEZ)

The Dow Jones U.S. Oil Equipment & Services Index Fund seeks investment results that correspond generally to the price and yield performance, before fees and expenses, of the Dow Jones U.S. Select Oil Equipment & Services Index

S&P Global Energy Sector Index Fund (IXC)

The S&P Global Energy Sector Index Fund seeks investment results that correspond generally to the price and yield performance, before fees and expenses, of companies that Standard & Poor's deems part of the energy sector of the economy and important to global markets, as represented by the S&P Global Energy Sector Index. The index is a subset of the Standard & Poor's Global 1200 Index.

PowerShares WilderHill Clean Energy (PBW)

The investment seeks investment results that correspond generally to the price and yield, before the Fund's fees and expenses, of the WilderHill Clean Energy Index. The Fund will normally invest at least 80% of its total assets in common stocks of companies engaged in the business of the advancement of cleaner energy and conservation. The Fund will normally invest at least 90% of its total assets in common stocks that comprise the Clean Energy Index.

There are also many mutual funds available whose objective is to invest in energy related investments. In selecting these mutual funds, as with any mutual fund, attention should be paid to the transaction, internal funds operating, and miscellaneous costs, as well as the longer term track record of the fund's managers.

The advantage of an ETF, or mutual fund, is that they offer broad, cost effective diversification within the energy sector. For investments in emerging areas and technologies, the benefits of trying to diversify away from the unique risks present is especially important. For example, alternative energy sources will play an increasingly important role in the global picture. As carbon based energy sources such as oil, gas, or coal become more expensive, alternative sources become much more attractive. There will not likely be just one replacement source of energy. There will be competing technologies and applications develop. It is impossible to definitively identify the ultimate victors to emerge from this process. For that reason, an ETF, like the Wilderhill Clean Energy Fund provides an opportunity to participate in an emerging growth area while, at the same time, offering cost effective diversification within this area.

For the investor willing to do more leg work or for a smaller portion of your overall investment allocation to energy related investments, there are also individual companies in which to invest. Some of these companies provide very attractive monthly income distributions. There are a number of companies organized as royalty income trusts which have monthly payouts over 10% on an annualized basis. Some examples of well established and well performing companies such as this would be:

- **Enerplus Resources (ERF)**. Enerplus Resources Fund operates as an energy investment trust in Western Canada. The fund, through its subsidiaries, engages in acquiring, exploiting, and operating crude oil and natural gas assets. Its oil and natural gas property interests are located in the provinces of British Columbia, Alberta, Saskatchewan, and Manitoba, in western Canada; and Montana and North Dakota, in the United States. As of December 31, 2005, the company had interests in the oil and natural gas property, which were estimated to contain proved plus probable reserves of 177.9 MMbbls of crude oil and NGLs, 53.2 MMbbls of bitumen and 1,308.3 Bcf of natural gas for a total of 449.1 MMBOE. Enerplus was founded in 1986 and is headquartered in Calgary, Canada. As of the middle of 2006, its monthly payout yield was over 7.5%. A very nice feature of this investment has been that in addition to a very nice income stream, it has also provided a hefty capital gain through share price appreciation.

- **Pengrowth Energy Trust (PGH)**. Pengrowth Energy Trust operates as a closed-end investment trust. The trust, through its subsidiary, Pengrowth Corporation, engages in the acquisition, ownership, and management of working interests and royalty interests in oil and natural gas properties and processing facilities in Canada. As of December 31, 2005, the company had proved plus probable reserves of 219,396 thousands of barrels of oil equivalent. The trust, formerly Pengrowth Gas Income Fund, was founded in 1988 and changed its name to Pengrowth Energy Trust in 1996. Pengrowth Energy trust is headquartered in Calgary, Canada. As of the middle of 2006, the monthly payment yield for Pengrowth was over 11%, annualized, while also providing good appreciation in its shares price.

- **BP Prudhoe Bay Royalty Trust (BPT).** With a monthly annualized yield of over 13% as of mid 2006, BP Prudhoe Bay Royalty Trust operates as a grantor trust. It holds overriding royalty interests constituting a non-operational interest in minerals in the Prudhoe Bay oil field located on the North Slope in Alaska. The Prudhoe Bay field extends approximately twelve miles by twenty-seven miles containing approximately 150,000 productive acres. The royalty interests entitle the trust to a royalty on 16.4246% of the first 90,000 barrels of the average actual daily net production of oil and condensate per quarter. The trust was founded in 1989 and is based in New York City.

Note that for all individual investments there are unique factors and risks which should be considered in determining how much, in any, of your investment allocations should be allocated to it. A 13% annualized yield may is attractive.

However, BP Royalty Trust also provides a good example of the unique risks involved with investing in an individual company. The money paid out from this company comes from 16.42% of the net proceeds from the first 90,000 barrels per day from B P Alaska's interest in the area. Along with other problems which appear to be cropping up with this company, production may be declining, as reported by Ellen McGirt of *Fortune* magazine in August, 2006. This could lead to a decline in revenue to be paid out.

Natural Resources and Commodities

Another investment area that lends itself to a similar analysis is investing in raw materials, commodities, and their related businesses. This would include copper, nickel, concrete, and all the other things which are required to build the cities, roads, and other infrastructure for the three billion, or so, people in the emerging economies of China and India. Aside from the huge demand these countries place upon these materials, we have also seen in our discussions of the geopolitical mega-trends, that many of the areas left with significant reserves of raw materials and natural resources are politically unstable, are remote and difficult to develop, and/or are not particularly favorably predisposed towards the United States. These are conditions which are likely to persist for some time. This means that those well managed companies, or investments, which offer investment exposure in these areas, have a high probability of performing well in the future. Consequently, they, too, deserve consideration for a place in the core positions of a mid to longer term investment portfolio.

There is risk in every opportunity. It is always a good idea to try to identify what changes could negatively impact the opportunities we have identified. The concerns that seem to have the most merit are of a global economic slowdown and/or political instability. These are certainly possible, and probably quite likely to occur. With China and India are growing their economies at 8-10% per year, how large of an economic slowdown would be necessary before we experienced a negative impact on the structural fundamentals of the investment opportunities discussed? If economic growth slowed to 0%, and we still had the current sustained consumption of these combined populations, we would still be seeing a very significant demand for energy and resources. It also appears that neither China nor India can politically afford the widespread economic disenchantment of their populations arising form stagnant economic growth. While probably not without some attention grabbing bumps on the road to continuing economic development, these countries have the political management of their populations at the top of their agendas. They are probably quite adept and competent as to their understanding, and ability, of what needs to be done for their political viability.

Within this same framework, agricultural firms would also appear to provide promising opportunities on several accounts. The three billion people of developing Asia, having more economic wherewithal with which to feed them, will create additional demand for agricultural products. At the same time, additional demand is being generated from the prospect of having basic food commodities, such as corn, sugar, and soybeans for use as biofuel energy sources, such as ethanol and biodiesel.

There are many investments which would fit within this framework. Some examples of these investments for positions in a longer term core portfolio positions would include:

Exchange Traded Funds iShares Goldman Sachs Natural Resources (IGE)

The Index includes companies in the following categories:

extractive industries, energy companies, owners of timber tracts, forestry services, producers of pulp and paper, and owners of plantations.

Dow Jones U.S. Basic Materials Sector Index Fund (IYM)

The index includes companies in the following sectors: chemicals, forestry and paper, industrial metals, and mining.

DB Commodity Index Tracking Fund (DBC)

The investment seeks to reflect the performance of the Deutsche Bank Liquid Commodity index. The fund will pursue its investment objective by investing in a portfolio of exchange-traded futures on the commodities comprising the index, or the index commodities. The index commodities are light, sweet crude oil, heating oil, aluminum, gold, corn, and wheat.

PowerShares Water Resources (PHO)

The index is comprised of twenty-five stocks of companies that are publicly traded in the U.S. and that focus on the provision of portable water, treatment of water, and technologies directly related to water consumption.

Mutual Funds

There are also numerous no-load mutual funds such as:

T. Rowe Price New Era Fund (PRNEX)

This no-load fund is in the common stocks of natural resource companies, which could benefit from accelerating inflation, as well as other growth companies that have strong potential for earnings growth but do not own or develop natural resources. The fund invests at least half of fund assets in U.S. securities, but invests up to 50% of assets in foreign securities.

U.S. Global Investors Global Resources (PSPFX)

The objective of this fund is for long-term growth of capital plus protection against inflation and monetary instability. It invests at least 80% of its assets in companies within the natural resource sector. It invests, without limitation, in the various industries of the natural resource sector, such as oil, gas, and basic materials.

Individual Stocks

Examples of individual stocks would include:

- **BHP Billiton**—an Australia based company founded in 1885. It is a mining company producing iron ore, copper, nickel metal, manganese, diamonds, silver, titanium, aluminum, and uranium. In addition, the company has ventures in the exploration, production, and development of oil and natural gas in Australia, the United Kingdom, the United States, Algeria, Trinidad and Tobago, and Pakistan. The company also exports metallurgical coal for the steel industry, and energy coal. It has exploration interests in the United States, Australia, Trinidad and Tobago, Pakistan, Algeria, Brunei Darussalam, South Africa, Canada, and the Philippines.

- **Phelps Dodge**—is a multi-national company with its headquarters in Phoenix, Arizona. Founded in 1834, it is a producer of copper, molybdenum, molybdenum-based chemicals, and continuous-cast copper rod worldwide. In addition to its operations in the United States, it has operations throughout the world. It also purchases and sells copper. It has a wire and cable division which manufactures magnet wire, copper, and aluminum energy cables; specialty conductors; and other products. Its products are sold to original equipment manufacturers for use in electrical motors, generators, transformers, medical applications, and public utilities in the United States, Latin America, Asia, and Africa.

- **Sadia**—While not a glamorous type business, this Brazilian company, founded in 1944, provides a staple as a refrigerated and frozen protein products company. It offers processed products, poultry, and pork. The company manufactures a range of processed products, including frozen products, such as hamburgers, breaded products, ready-made dishes, and pizzas; refrigerated products, including hams, sausages, frankfurters, bolognas, salamis, cold cuts, product portions, and refrigerated pasta; and margarine, primarily under the Sadia brand. It also breeds, slaughters, and distributes poultry, pork products, as well as beef. It offers its products through distribution and sales centers in the Middle East, Asia, South America, and Europe. A nice additional benefit of this company is that besides its favorable growth prospects, it also offers a nice dividend yield, which, at the time of this writing, is about 6%.

- **Cresud**—Another South American company, founded in 1936, and headquartered in Buenos Aires, Argentina, Cresud produces basic agricultural products. Its various operations and activities include crop production, beef-cattle production, and milk production. The company's crop production consists primarily of the sowing and harvesting of fine and coarse grains, and oilseeds. Its principal crops include wheat, corn, soybean, and sunflower; and other crops, such as sorghum. The company's beef-cattle production involves the raising and fattening of beef-cattle from its own stock for sale to slaughterhouses and supermarkets, in addition to producing milk. The company is also involved in real estate development and forestry activities. While still emerging from the collapse of its economy at the opening of the 21st Century, there are many potential values to be had in this region.

International Investments

If there is one conclusion which should be reached from our discussions of the mega-trends affecting your investments and personal finances, it is that the economy of the United States has many difficult challenges ahead. The astronomical budget deficits require a massive and growing debt, and the transference of the competitive advantage of many key industries in the United States has lead to a hemorrhaging of dollars to countries such as China, India, and the oil producing countries. An aging population, poorly prepared for their retirement years, can expect declining health and increasing claims on a Federal entitlement system which is seriously under funded relative to its Medicare liabilities, and Social Security can be considered marginally funded at best. Corruption, ethical malfeasance, and engagement in an endless war against a poorly defined enemy promises to continue draining the productive economic, emotional, and psychological resources of the United States. At the same time, the United States remains dependent for its energy supplies on countries and regions which do not look favorably upon the United States.

It is only reasonable and prudent for an investor to consider what investment environments, other than the United States, might provide more favorable opportunities. Technology and globalization has made investing throughout the world accessible to virtually any investor in the United States. While all investments have their own unique risks, neglecting to commit a core allocation of your investments outside of the United States is more than a missed opportunity; it is an error of judgment with regard to diversifying your risk.

Another way in which to capitalize on the profitability of natural resources, for example, is to consider investing in countries which have strong resource based economies. In particular, the economies of Canada, Australia, as well as a number of the Latin American countries can provide good opportunities if chosen wisely, and in moderation. One additional dimension of risk which needs to be considered is that in some other countries the rule of law as applied to property rights is more tenuous than in the United States. For example, Russia is also has a strong resource based economy. However, my observations at the whimsical manipulations of Putin leave me uneasy at the prospect that Russia may at any time decide it is in their interest to reallocate ownership of property according to their political agenda. We can make similar observations in some Latin American countries, such as Bolivia's inclination to renationalize the ownership of their mining and energy sectors. The question becomes how to manage the risk in these investments. Depending upon your risk tolerances and preferences, the fundamental way in which to manage these risks is by limiting the exposure you have to them. This can be done by the percentage of your funds you have allocated as well as by diversifying among the geographical regions, as well as the companies within these regions. Exchange Traded Funds and mutual funds are one cost effective method of accomplishing this objective.

A few examples of Exchange Traded Funds which will accomplish this objective are:

iShares MSCI Canada Index (EWC)

The investments within this fund include an allocation of over 30% to energy related companies, over 16% each to materials and banks. Such companies as Royal Bank of Canada, Manulife Financial, Suncor Energy, and EnCana Corporation are held in its portfolio.

MSCI Australia Index Fund (EWA)

This fund provides and opportunity to gain investment exposure in a country that is well positioned geographically to capitalize on the rapid economic development of Asia, as well as being able to offer exposure to a resource rich economy. Besides the strong natural resource base of this economy, the financial sector has benefited, as well, from the country's proximity to Asia similar to the Canadian fund, the rule of law defining and protecting property rights, as well as relative political stability limiting the investment risk in these areas of investing outside of the United States. Companies such as BHP Billiton, Ltd., one of the largest mining companies in the world, and Rio Tinto, as well as Rio Tinto, produce aluminum, copper, diamonds, energy products, gold, and iron ore.

MSCI Brazil Index Fund (EWZ)

Investing in Latin America provides exposure to natural resource rich and rapidly growing economies. Developing favorable relationships with Russia and China suggest that growth will continue, even in the event of an economic slowdown in the United States. The problem with Latin America is unstable government and unfavorable views towards the United States. While not without problems, the economy of Brazil holds the promise of being at the top echelon of global economies. In addition to having an abundance of the world's needed natural resources, Brazil is also an agricultural powerhouse. This index fund has over 25% of its funds allocated to materials related investments, and close to 25% in energy related investments.

Precious Metals

A very influential economist of the early twentieth century, John Maynard Keynes, called gold a barbarous relic as an expression of his disdain for what had been accepted for thousands of years as a form of money. If gold were really a barbarous relic, one has to question why central banks of the world hold such huge bullion reserves in their treasuries. Could it be the belief of these central bankers that gold still serves the fundamental purpose of money as a store of value? Whatever the reason is, there are many good reasons to hold investments in gold, as well as other precious metals, as a core portfolio position. The reasons serve both as a defensive measure and as a potential source of exceptional future growth.

We have seen how the astronomical budget deficits of the United States have grown out of control. Given the prospects of continuing and growing financial commitments to social entitlement programs, national defense expenditures, unexpected contingencies like national disaster response, as well as the myriad of other issues discussed more fully in previous chapters, a conscientious investor must consider how the United States will deal with this budgetary debacle. One tool governments have exclusive claim to is the ability to create money. Note that creating money is not the same as creating value. When money is created without a commensurate increase in value, money is effectively devalued. This strategy is called monetizing the debt. If you can imagine having to take a wheel barrel full of currency to purchase your weekly groceries, as in Germany before the Second World War, you can get a picture of an example of hyperinflation. You can see that the creation of money without the creation of value puts a lot of currency in circulation with which to pay a fixed, existing debt. This is another way of devaluing the dollar. An investor's holding position dependent upon the value of the dollar and what it can purchase would be in serious peril. If you consider the trillions of dollar-denominated investments held by central banks, institutions, and petro-interests, it would be a serious under-estimation of their financial competency to believe these investors would not think of finding other places to retain the value of their wealth.

Gold and other precious metals have already seen increasing investor interest. In addition to the defensive nature of having some percentage allocation to gold, the increased purchasing power of Asia has also increased demand for gold in economies like India, and China. If for nothing else than insurance against an exodus from the dollar, these investments should be in the portfolio of even the conservative investor. Depending upon how much in jeopardy you believed the United States financial system to be, a greater percentage allocation to these investments may provide a unique growth opportunity to the more aggressive or speculative investor. My view is that at least a 10% diversified position in precious metals is prudent for most investors. Investments can be made in this area through the direct purchase of the metals themselves, which leads to a storage problem. It can also be invested through funds which have direct ownership of the metal, and provide for storage and insurance, or you can hold investments in mining companies. If investing directly in individual mining companies, one needs to do the necessary homework on the company. There is a saying that many gold mining companies can be characterized by the saying that a gold mining company is "a hole in the ground with a liar standing over it". In effect, there are many good gold mining investments, but there are also many that are not good risks.

Some examples of diversified approaches to investing in precious metals are:

iShares Comex Gold Trust (IAU)

This is a cost effective way to invest in the direct ownership of gold without the concern about the storage and insurance of it. The objective of the Gold Trust is for the value to reflect, at any given time, the price of gold owned by the Gold Trust at that time, less the expenses and liabilities of the Gold Trust. As of the middle of September, 2006, it owned over forty-three tons of gold. As new money is invested in the fund, it purchases additional gold.

iShares Silver Trust (SLV)

Operating in a similar way as the **Gold Trust** discussed above, this trust purchases, stores, and insures silver for its investors.

Market Vectors Gold Miners ETF(GDX)

This is an exchange traded funded developed by the Van Eck mutual fund family. It is designed to track the Amex Gold Miners Index. It is diversified by company size and geographic location among gold mining companies, including approximately forty-five different companies.

Defense

Unfortunate as the case may be, our discussion of geopolitics and terrorism strongly suggests that military engagements will be a regular part of our reality for many years to come. War and security appear to be growth industries. This is an industry sector which will be somewhat resistant to a downturn in global economic conditions. If anything, war and military conflict have seemed to serve the political purpose diverting people's attention from the personal deteriorating financial conditions of their lives. In looking for a common enemy upon which to blame these circumstances, we might expect even more military engagement and conflict as economic conditions deteriorate. In the book <u>Resource Wars</u> by Michael Klare, the case is made that the scarcity of resources has been, and will be, a leading cause of war. This point has also been made by Marc Faber, a noted speaker at investment symposiums, and author of <u>Tomorrow's Gold</u>. In a webcast presentation for the mutual fund family, US Global Investors, Inc., he made the point that the increasing scarcity of strategic resources, because of rising demand and constrained supply, has put the world on a course for greater military conflict. Those investors, who are willing to invest in the defense industry, may profit substantially from this weakness of the human condition. Some examples of investments in this area are:

Dow Jones U.S. Aerospace & Defense Index Fund (ITA)

This exchange traded fund has approximately 55% of its investments in the aerospace industry and 45% in the defense industry. Among the top ten companies comprising this index fund are United Technologies Corporation, Boeing, Lockheed Martin Corporation, and General Dynamics.

A no-load mutual fund also investing in the defense sector is:

Fidelity Select Defense & Aerospace (FSDAX)

Stylistically, this mid-cap, blend fund invests around 80% of assets in companies engaged in the research, manufacture, or sale of products or services related to the defense or aerospace industries. It may invest in securities of foreign issuers.

Investments Likely to Be Extremely Hazardous to Your Financial Health

We have looked at a number of promising investments areas based upon the global investment landscape discussed in the first part of this book. While it important in the investment management process to identify promising areas of opportunity, it is also important to identify investment areas which may be particularly hazardous in order to reduce our exposure to them, or avoid them entirely. The areas which seem particularly vulnerable, based upon the mega-trends we discussed, are in the financial sector-banks, insurance companies, brokerages, residential housing, and despite the conventional beliefs on the subject, healthcare.

The financial system is a house of cards. It has been propped up by easy credit created by artificially induced low interest rates. As we have seen, the level of governmental and personal indebtedness has grown to astronomical proportions and cannot continue in this direction indefinitely. The circumstances of our financial system are comparable to building a magnificent house on a rotting foundation. The likely result will be that sooner or later the structure will collapse, unless repairable. The evidence we have gathered in our book suggests that the problem may well be beyond constructive resolution. Compounding these circumstances are the unknown contingent financial stresses of institutional malfeasance, or the costs of coping with natural disasters, as well as the demands placed upon the economic system with an aging population of declining productivity. This will require more social assistance through costly and under funded entitlement programs. Any number of events could create a serious crisis in this house of cards. Most vulnerable will be the financial institutions, such as banks, which depend upon borrower's willingness to borrow and ability to repay.

Along these same lines is a glut in housing inventory, also stimulated by the easy credit of artificially low interest costs. This will likely be compounded by an increasing supply of additional housing inventory entering the market as owners are squeezed by economic circumstances into foreclosures. It would not appear that home builders, or other residential construction related industries, including mortgage related businesses, would offer particularly favorable investment opportunities, at least in the near future.

Moving on to the healthcare sector, the popular wisdom is that because of the increasing demand for healthcare by the demographics of an aging and increasingly unhealthy population, healthcare is assumed to be a good investment for the future. The problem, however, as I see it, is that despite the demand for these services, in order to have profitable businesses, there must be the ability to pay for these services. As we have seen in our documented discussion on this subject, the increasing costs of our healthcare system are not sustainable. The political and economic realities suggest a crisis point will be reached, probably within the near future, which will precipitate a change in the system. More than likely, the political pressures will generate some sort of regulatory intervention. Inevitably, this will be some sort of cost containment system. The result will be a curtailment of the profitability generally expected of the healthcare sector.

CHAPTER NINE
Part Two
Portfolio Construction Strategy

Portfolio Construction

We have looked at the global landscape of mega-trends that are shaping the economic and investment environment. Because of the magnitude of these events, these trends will continue in the future. We have also looked at specific investment areas, some of which look very promising in this environment, and some of which should be avoided. A sound investment strategy, however, is more than identifying promising investments to consider and hazardous investments to avoid. It involves more than having a grasp of the events impacting your investments. A sound investment strategy also must take into consideration targeted and realistic financial objectives. This, in turn, should drive the construction of a portfolio having specific allocations to the investments suggested by a sound analysis of the major forces of impact.

It is beyond the scope of this book to delve into the intricacies, or critiques, of Modern Portfolio Theory. There are, however, a number of concepts which will probably be intuitively acceptable to most investors. One of these concepts is the relationship between potential risk and reward. In well—developed financial markets there is relative market efficiency in which a quest for higher investment returns means assuming greater risks. Optimizing an investment portfolio means striving to attain the best potential reward for a given level of risk, or alternatively minimizing the risk for a given level of expected reward. When realistic financial objectives drive portfolio construction, managing the risk associated with investing becomes a more definable and manageable task.

In over sixteen years of working with clients, I have never had someone identify their financial objective as dying with as much money as possible. For most people, objectives such as having a comfortable life, pre- and post retirement, funding children's college educations, or even leaving a charitable legacy are more what is important. These are generally quantifiable objectives. With financial planning, current and future resources can be estimated using what appear to be reasonable assumptions. Consideration of personal preferences, inflation and tax expectations can lead to a rate of investment return needed to attain your financial objectives. If reasonable, based upon historical evidence, market conditions, and the level of risk associated with this rate of investment return we would have guidance as to how many dollars to allocate to specific investments.

There are innumerable theories on how to construct investment portfolios. Over the years, I have looked at many of these approaches. While I don't believe there is any perfect approach, two models which have the merit of at least providing a systematic and disciplined approach are asset allocation, and the core and satellite model. We will discuss each of these.

Asset Allocation

Asset allocation has become a buzzword in the financial services lexicon. Stock brokers, financial planners, money managers, insurance agents, and estate planners all use the term asset allocation. While the basic concepts of asset allocation are based upon the mathematically and empirically rigorous academic work of Modern Portfolio theory, its use has been highly commercialized. A good part of the reason for this is that asset allocation models give the impression of being a mechanical process, whereby, with a minimal amount of thought and critical analysis, a formula is provided for investment success. The simplicity of this approach, at least at the surface level, makes it an easier sell to many investors who don't have the time, patience, or background to delve into the issues that are really likely to impact their investment success. The mathematics behind asset allocation has also made it a very programmable system for software development. There are many software programs, or websites, that offer asset allocation services. The impression with which one is left after using some of these programs is that asset allocation is a precision science whereby one can calculate to within one hundredth of one percent the amount of risk and expected return of a given portfolio. Even many financial advisors with whom I have spoken at professional conferences are of this belief, asset allocation is not, however, a precision science. It is an erroneous belief to attribute an engineering precision and predictive power to the results of asset allocation, even when done correctly. This is not to say that asset allocation does not provide a useful structure for an investor. If an investor is to increase the chances of a successful outcome, however, it is important to recognize the limits of the tools that are being used. Asset allocation is a tool, and it has its limitations.

The work often cited in discussions about asset allocation are a couple of studies done by Brinson, Singer and Beebower, called "The Determinants of Portfolio Performance," Financial Analysts Journal, July-Aug. 1986; and "Determinants of Portfolio Performance II: An Update," Financial Analysts Journal, May-June 1991. The conclusion reached was that the major determinant of a portfolio's investment performance was not the specific investments in that portfolio, but rather the asset classes that were represented. Asset classes are groupings of investments which have some similar predefined characteristics. Some examples of asset classes would be stock, bonds, real estate, and cash. These can, of course, be further broken down. For example, we could break down stocks into small cap, mid cap, large cap, domestic, foreign, etc. We could even further break these down into additional asset classes representing industry sectors, specific foreign geographical regions, etc.

The idea behind asset allocation is that by studying past historical behaviors and inter-relationships between asset classes, we can find such information as historical average annual investment performance, as well as what the probability and expected variation (or risk) might be from this average from year to year. In addition, and very important for asset allocation, we can study how the results from one asset class are correlated with the result of another asset class. The idea is that if we can find asset classes that are negatively correlated with one another, meaning when one goes up, the other goes down, we can blend these various asset classes together in innumerable different combinations to get different risk/reward profiles for hypothetical portfolios. The use of computers allows an effective and efficient method of combining vast numbers of hypothetical portfolios very quickly.

For the naïve user of asset allocation, which also includes many financial sales representatives, there is a tendency to be awed by the precision type results which emerge from such an analysis. It should be noted, however, that despite the prevalent use of these asset allocation models, this methodology is not without it critics. There is serious professional discussion and debate regarding the merits of asset allocation. From my perspective, regardless of its potential utility, I see both theoretical and practical deficiencies in the asset allocation model.

From a practical point of view, we have seen how asset classes can be sub-divided into smaller asset classes and studied. The more potential asset classes we have, the greater the number of potential portfolio combinations we can create, the greater our investment universe, and the more effectively we can create risk/reward efficient portfolios. Many of the asset allocation programs and services use relatively few asset classes; other, more sophisticated programs may use a great number of them. How many various asset classes and which ones to use are poorly defined, and from my perspective, an open question.

Additionally, the question of the best way to implement an asset allocation strategy is also a question which, in my experience, has not been adequately addressed. Let's say that you have a lump sum of money to invest. Do you develop an asset allocation strategy and then invest all of this lump sum into the recommended allocations? If so, this strategy seems to leave much to be desired, sometimes, much more so than others. The idea behind asset allocation is that some asset classes are going up while others are going down. This means that at some point the asset classes in an asset allocation strategy would have some investments represented at their higher points, others at their lower points. In general, these variations may not be significant over time. However, let's consider the case where there may be extreme variations of asset class performance. As one example, let's consider the case of bonds and interest rates.

Bonds and interest rates generally work inversely with one another; that is, decreasing interest rates drive bond prices lower and increasing interest rates drive bond prices higher. The mathematical analysis of why this occurs is interesting, but beyond the scope of our work here. If we are in an economic environment with historically low interest rates, and our analysis of the economic environment suggests a high probability of interest rates increasing, perhaps significantly, an investment in bonds at a time like this would be asking to lose money.

The asset allocation strategies I have seen, particularly those designed for the conservative investor, usually have bonds as a designated asset class within which to invest. The strategies are usually silent on the issues such as extremes in the current market cycles, including interest rates, stock, or bond prices. The mechanical nature of this investment approach would have us believe that these things do not matter. This is more akin to faith-based investing as opposed to a thoughtful analysis. An intuitive and intelligent analysis would conclude that these things most certainly do matter. Hence, while an asset allocation approach can provide a relatively disciplined and structured approach to creating a portfolio, the indiscriminate and less sophisticated approaches may actually be harmful to your financial health.

While I intend this work to be of a more practical nature, it is appropriate at least to refer to some of the more theoretical deficiencies, which I believe need be addressed in the asset allocation approach. As an example, a fundamental concept behind asset allocation has to do with how different asset classes are correlated with one another. There are a number of open questions in deriving these correlations. How far back in time do we go to gather the information used in deriving our asset class correlations, expected average investment returns, and variations from these returns? Do we give equal weighting to performance characteristics from thirty years ago as we do to more recent performance and asset class behaviors? How do globalization, technological change, and governmental economic intervention affect the correlations between asset classes? As we can see, there are many open, and relevant, questions which are replaced by nothing more than assumptions in the generally accepted asset allocation approaches.

Additional considerations, from a personal financial planning perspective, are:

What is your investment time horizon?

What are your financial objectives?

What are your cash flow needs?

How much risk can you tolerate, psychologically, emotionally, and materially?

What are your overall financial resources?

The bottom line, in my opinion, is that if the structure of the asset allocation model is to be used as an investment strategy, its implementation should at least be informed by the existing economic and investment landscape, as well as personal needs. The mega-trends discussed in this book are, I believe, some of the major areas which should be considered in the guiding of this informing process.

Core & Satellite Portfolio Approach

Although this approach to portfolio construction may be one that most retail investors have never heard of, it has been around for quite some time among institutional type investors. The typical approach to this type of portfolio construction is to combine both a passive and active approach to investment management. The passive component of the portfolio is comprised of index type investments. These are unmanaged "baskets" of stocks having the characteristic defined by the index. For example, we could have an index of small, midsize, or large companies in our index. Alternatively we could have an index representing an industry sector such as energy, real estate, or mining. We could even have indexes of bonds of various sorts. If you are starting to think this sounds an awful lot like asset classes, you are getting the idea. A central idea behind this index type investing is that because investment markets are so efficient, it is difficult for more active managers to outperform an unmanaged index. Because of the passive nature of these indexes, they also have the additional advantage of having lower internal management costs, lower transaction fees, as well as greater tax efficiency. Using this model, these indexes would form the core of our investment portfolio.

In the typical core and satellite model, the core investment positions would represent a broad index of stocks, such as the S&P 500, which represents the 500 largest companies from various industries of the United States. In this case the investor is saying that they wish do just as well as this broader index, no better, no worse. The satellite component of this type of portfolio would be more actively selected and managed. The intent with the active component is to boost the overall portfolio return with the better than average performance of these satellite positions. If, on the other hand, they perform worse than average, then the investor has limited exposure, and consequently risk that is limited by to the amount invested in these investments. You might liken it to trying to get a little extra octane in an investment tank with these satellite additives.

It should be kept in mind, however, that the core and satellite approach, as with any portfolio development approach, does not eliminate risk. It is just one way of managing risk. The core position, while representing a well diversified allocation to specific investment areas, may eliminate, or reduce the unique risk of any individual investment. It is still subject to the systematic risk of the entire asset classes represented. It will still be subject to some degree of volatility. The components of these core portfolio positions can be allocated as to create a higher or lesser degree of risk and reward. A conservative investor may want to stabilize these core positions with a larger cash position and/or larger allocations to relatively safe investments such as short-term United States Treasury Bills. These have a very short time frame for maturity, a very low risk that the creditor, the United States government, will default on repayment, and a very small risk that interest rate changes will severely impair your investment. An exchange traded fund (ETF) such as one investing only in short-term United States Treasury Debt could also be used. One perspective of this core and satellite approach would be to consider the core investments providing the basic flavor of the portfolio, or the center of gravity of the portfolio.

A more aggressive investor could choose core positions which would have greater potential return as well as greater potential risk. The risk/reward profile could also be adjusted by the size of the core relative to the overall portfolio. For example, an investor could choose core investments representing diversified indexes of smaller, emerging market, and speculative stocks to represent 75% of the overall portfolio, The balance of the portfolio, might be in something relatively safe with a lower expected return, such as for example United States Treasury Bills. One would reasonably expect greater volatility on a portfolio such as this, with the relatively safe satellite position of U.S. Treasuries providing somewhat of a smoothing effect to the overall performance. The idea is that depending upon what your needs and risk tolerance is, you target an investment return from your portfolio that will allow you to be successful in reaching your financial objective.

Changes would be made to these positions only after careful analysis indicating the desirability of such a structural change. Consequently the initial commitment to these investment positions should be based upon trends which can be expected to persist over the near future, such as the ones discussed earlier in this book. If the strategic vision guiding the selection of these investment positions is based upon sustainable structural trends, then the variations in the performance of these core investments should viewed as market noise or the investment cyclicality within a much stronger trend.

Choice of the core components of this type of portfolio is of utmost importance. In my opinion, these investments should reflect the best long term opportunities that can be reasonable identified. The ideas discussed in this book were intended to highlight these areas.

From my perspective, I prefer to view the core component of this strategy as providing the component of stability. Therefore, I prefer the low volatility type of investment such as the Treasury Bills, short-term, high credit quality bonds, and, yes, even cash type investments such as money markets funds. These investments are relatively low yielding, but safe type investments. I use the satellite components of this portfolio strategy to provide the extra boost needed for a targeted investment return intended to meet a financial objective.

As a consequence, let's take a look at what a hypothetical investment portfolio might look like for an investor with a moderate risk tolerance and growth needs, based upon the areas of long-term opportunity suggested by earlier chapters.

Core Positions

Short Term US Treasuries,
Money Markets, CD's, etc.   35%

Satellite Positions

Gold & Precious Metals   10%
Gold & silver mining companies,

bullion, uranium, platinum,
palladium, etc.

Natural Resources/Basic Materials	10%
Mining, timber, water resources, etc.	
Energy Related	10%
Oil related, alternative energy, etc.	
International Regions	30%
China, India, Brazil, etc.	
Open to Opportunities	5%

Shifting the amounts from the satellite positions into the core position would result in a more conservative portfolio allocation to the more risk adverse investor. The specific investments to fill these broader asset class allocations can be from exchange traded funds (ETF's) or from low cost mutual funds providing representation in these areas. Note that having some investment representation from the defense industry would also likely be profitable if chosen wisely.

I should also point out that cash, in the form of money market funds, certificate of deposits, savings, or checking accounts have their valid place in a portfolio. There are times when holding a larger cash type position is a wise investment choice.

This hypothetical portfolio is provided as an example to represent the ideas in this book. Rather than being prescriptive in nature, the intent of this book has been to provide a way of thinking about how to make investment and financial planning decisions in the context of the very real issues that are and will be impacting our lives in the near future. Unfortunately, the world in which we live does not realistically lend itself to the simplicity of a neat formula or mechanical approach. In my opinion, those investors who are seduced by the notion of type of simplicity and institutional assurances are placing their faith in a system which does not have their particular interests in mind. There will be no substitute for an informed and critical approach to thinking about making financial decisions.

Understanding that not everyone has the interest, time, energy, or desire to develop the expertise needed, the next step would be to identify advisors who can provide objective advice from an independent perspective, who seem to be aware, knowledgeable, and responsive to the issues we have discussed. Their primary professional objective should be to work in your interest, you the client. Having a basic fundamental understanding, such as that provided by this book should serve as a guide to either developing this critical expertise yourself, or alternatively being able to screen potential advisors on their understanding and awareness of the issues.